Raising
Courageous
Kids

To Erica
For all the courage
you have discovered
and all the courage
you will inspire!

Charles A. Smith
So nice to meet
your mom at
NAEYC

Eight Steps to Practical Heroism

Raising
Courageous
Kids

Charles A. Smith

SORIN BOOKS Notre Dame, Indiana

www.sorinbooks.com

International Standard Book Number 1-893732-76-2

Cover and text design by Katherine Robinson Coleman

Printed and bound in the United States of America.

Library of Congress Cataloging-in-Publication Data

Smith, Charles A.

  Raising courageous kids : eight steps to practical heroism / Charles A. Smith.

    p. cm.

  Includes bibliographical references (p.).

  ISBN 1-893732-76-2 (pbk.)

  1. Courage. 2. Child rearing. I. Title.

BF723.C694S63 2004

649'.7--dc22

2004008605

Contents

For Sarah and Bill

Acknowledgments

My thanks go first to my mother, Ann Sanborn Fadie, whose love during my childhood gave me strength and taught me of the importance of caring.

My thanks, too, to Miriam Tager, my agent at the Nancy Love Literary Agency. Miriam's encouragement replaced the solitude of "me" with the enthusiasm of "we." Her patient support in the crafting of the proposal for *Raising Courageous Kids* gave a great boost to this work and made its publication possible.

I enjoyed the opportunity to team up once again with Myrna Daly, who contributed her copyediting expertise in preparing the final draft of the manuscript.

I am also grateful for the information and support provided by Douglas Chambers, managing director of the Carnegie Hero Commission. The work of the Commission has been an inspiration to me as I planned and wrote this book. I stand in awe of the recipients of the Carnegie Hero Medal and hope in at least some small way to honor their courage.

I was fortunate to find a partnership with the fine professionals at Sorin Books who believed in *Raising Courageous Kids* and so ably shepherded the book from proposal to reality. I especially appreciate the expert assistance of Mike Amodei and Geri Pawelski.

My friends and colleagues at Kansas State University, including Charlotte Olsen, Bill Meredith, Nancy Peterson, Terrie McCants, Steve Bollman, Mike Bradshaw, and Paula Seele, offered encouragement and showed faith in the significance of my work.

Wally Goddard, a talented professional whose work and playfulness I much admire, provided a reassuring voice that continues to enrich my life.

To bridge the gap between imagination and accomplishment I benefited from the support of my family. Sarah and Bill Smith graciously allowed me to share my experiences of their childhood with readers. Sarah provided invaluable suggestions for improving the manuscript. Evidence of her delightful way with words can be found throughout this book. I am also thankful to my wife Betsy for being my companion on this journey.

Finally I would like to thank all the wonderful children I taught during my years as a preschool teacher. My experiences with them continue to provide a rich source of insight.

—Charles A. Smith
Manhattan, Kansas

Children,
Our Heart Work

On August 18, 2001, an alligator attacked Edna Wilkes as she and a group of other fourteen-year-old boys and girls floated on boogie boards in a Florida canal. As her friends frantically paddled to shore, the alligator pulled Edna under the water, spinning her in a churning whirlpool. Fighting desperately to escape, she managed to free herself from the alligator's jaws. When she surfaced, Edna was alone—almost. Everyone had fled except for Amanda Valance.

Amanda helped Edna—fainting, losing blood, and crippled by a broken arm—onto the boogie board. Then she pulled her thirty feet to shore, a distance that the injured girl could not have reached alone. By the time she arrived at the hospital, Edna's blood pressure was undetectable. She narrowly survived the attack.

What made Amanda stay in the water to help her friend when everyone else fled? From her hospital bed, Edna reported that Amanda said she "saw his tail whipping around in the water, and she . . . thought to herself she couldn't let me die." When Amanda recalled the horrible moment, she reported, "For five split seconds, I felt like I had to leave, *but I could not do that to her.*"

Three weeks later, duty, courage, and heroism were demonstrated on a greater scale on the streets of New York, at the Pentagon in Washington, D.C., and in the skies over Pennsylvania. Stories like Amanda's were repeated hundreds of times on September 11, 2001. Courage born of desperation was evident everywhere that day:

- Firefighters, rescue personnel, and police officers rushed *up* the steps of the World Trade Center while office workers fled *down* to safety.

- A fire department chaplain was killed by falling debris while mimistering to the injured.

- An office worker stayed behind with an injured colleague; both perished in the collapse of the towers.

- Two men helped a woman in a wheelchair down sixty-eight floors to safety as one of the towers disintegrated behind them.

- Passengers on United Flight 93 drew from strength deep within their hearts, took fate into their own hands, and rose from their seats to resist their hijackers.

- Custodians at the Pentagon risked their lives in flooded hallways to shut down electrical generators.

John Cerqueira, one of the rescuers of the wheelchair-bound woman, later said, "In the back of my head I could hear my mother telling me to get the heck out of there. *But I had to help.*" John's words are remarkably similar to Amanda Valance's declaration, "*. . . but I could not do that to her.*" These words reveal the true nature of the heroic heart, one that resonates with power, caring, vigilance, and composure. What can we hope to learn from any tragedy in which cruelty and indifference to suffering cause immense shock and profound heartbreak? Tragic circumstances provide opportunities for heroic action. Every act of heroism teaches us that courage and caring are possible in the worst of circumstances. Our responsibility is to learn from those who take risks and make sacrifices on behalf of others and to ensure that lessons of true heroism are understood by the next generation. Children depend on us, their parents and teachers, to help them find the tenacity to face fear, the endurance to struggle against adversity, and the commitment to respond to suffering.[1]

We are not born heroes. The journey to find courage begins at birth. As the seed of courage begins to grow, young children discover their emerging power, influence, and capacity for love. As they continue to mature, fear will force them to make a choice between retreating and advancing. A courageous response to adversity will give their lives strength, much like a drought forces the roots of a tree to go deeper into the ground to find moisture. The deeper the roots of courage, the stronger they become: the tree with shallow roots is more easily uprooted in a storm.

There may come a time when our children will face a great test. Like the courageous people described in this book, they may witness a desperate plea for help or face adversity that threatens their survival. This test may occur suddenly, without warning, or approach relentlessly as a continuing hardship. They will need resilience, intelligence, and grace to make wise choices.

Parents serve as guides who blaze the path to courage, demonstrating perseverance, intelligent problem solving, and the impulse to aid others. They encourage children to keep trying when they face obstacles, and read or tell stories of magnificent deeds that inspire them. *Raising Courageous Kids: Eight Steps to Practical Heroism* is a map to assist you in blazing the trail to courage with children.

Greatness requires bravery

We love our children for who they are; yet we hope our children will achieve the greatness of their potential. We see hints occasionally of what they may become—scientists, explorers, artists. We imagine them growing up to become good people and, we hope, to achieve something special.

Great accomplishments require courage—overcoming fear to persevere. No real achievement can be made without making sacrifices or taking risks. Martin Luther King Jr., Cesar Chavez, and Mother Teresa achieved greatness because they did not to allow fear to determine their course of action. Furthermore, they elevated their courage to the level of heroism by striving for noble goals on behalf of others.

Great accomplishments do not always result in fame. Courage exists all around us—in our communities, in our children's schools, and in our homes:

- Across town, a single mother dying from a brain tumor builds a legacy of love and devotion in her relationship with her young daughter.

- Across the street, a child with cystic fibrosis, a terminal disease involving a lifetime of intensive physical therapy, faces her daily struggle with grace and determination.

- Next door, a young teen finds the power to stand up to the torments of a bully on the school bus.

Each person displays courage that is neither trumpeted in newspaper headlines nor celebrated on Main Street by marching bands and cheering crowds. Their victories are recorded where they are the most important—in the hearts and minds of their families. Heroism is displayed by regular people who have risen to the challenge of fear. As Hubert Humphrey wrote, "American democracy is based upon the belief that there are extraordinary possibilities in ordinary people." Every act of heroism is evidence of this truth. By nurturing courage in our children, we make it possible for them to achieve greatness.

Risk and sacrifice are a part of life

No matter how much we try to protect our children, hardship and misfortune will be a part of their journey. Adults are not always available to help. Responding to adversity always involves risk. Imagine how you would like your children to respond in the following circumstances:

- A classmate deliberately hurts your preschooler.

- A bully demands that your eight-year-old hand over her lunch money.

- An older boy tries to force your twelve-year-old daughter to drink, use drugs, or have sex.

In many circumstances, we cannot be physically present to lend a supporting hand or whisper an encouraging word. Will our children have the courage to stand up for themselves and the wisdom to make smart choices when faced with difficult situations? Will they be active rather than passive, despite risk?

To retreat in the face of danger has consequences, too. What happens to our children when they fail to stand up to bullies? Or resist the threats of predators? They too become victims and invite additional misery into their lives. Only thoughtful courage will enable our children to thrive.

Children today grow up more afraid than they did in the classic carefree childhood of the recent past. Kaoru Yamamoto of the University of Colorado examined how stressful various events were rated by elementary schoolchildren. The six top fears of sixth-graders were losing a parent, going blind, being held back a year in school, wetting their pants in school, hearing parents quarrel, and being caught stealing something. These fears are shared by children at this age around the world.[2]

The moment they leave our doorsteps, our children face adversity without our shield. We have the responsibility to prepare them to make decisions for when they are out on their own.

Courage is an essential virtue

Courage is more than an attitude that we depend on when danger approaches. Courage is a catalyst, a keystone virtue that boosts all of our other positive human qualities. Winston Churchill wrote, "Courage is the first of human qualities because it is the quality that guarantees all the other things."

For example, faith and hope can only be sustained by courage. Love and generosity require courage. Courage is the mother tree of virtue, providing nourishment to its branches of faith, hope, love, and integrity. Courage invests all positive qualities with vitality that underlies growth. Without courage, our best potential will wither and die.

Nobility builds strong communities

Imagine being physically assaulted in public, surrounded by onlookers who refuse to intervene. Imagine passing out or being overcome by illness while shopping and being ignored by onlookers. Imagine that your car turns over in an accident and, when flames appear, those nearby are unwilling to take the risk of pulling you out. What would life be like in such a community?

Courage provides the ethical backbone for a community. Courageous citizens in healthy communities oppose any force, no matter how powerful, that degrades their quality of life. They take responsibility for ensuring that their neighborhoods are safe. Children attend schools without fear. Families gather at neighborhood playgrounds. Every person knows that in his or her time of need neighbors and strangers will be there to help.

Communities ruled by fear are dead and lifeless. People continue to live in them, but only as fleeting ghosts, insubstantial and unseen. In contrast, communities based on courage have vitality. They prosper because their citizens care and find strength in their union.

The commitment to courage

A national renewed commitment to courage and heroism is the best response to the challenges we face. A Time/CNN poll found that eight months after the tragedy on September 11, 2001, nearly two-thirds of Americans think about the terror attacks at least several times a week.[3] Fear of terrorism adds to the list of our anxieties: school violence, child abduction, economic decline, and a host of other everyday dangers lurking around the corner. The cover of a June 2002 issue of *Time* magazine declared "Understanding anxiety: Now more than ever we are worrying ourselves sick."

Children feel the weight of fear as well. In 1997, 23 percent of ninth graders reported having carried a weapon in the previous thirty days, twice the number of twelfth graders who had armed themselves during the same time.[4] The National Association of School Psychologists reported on a study of sixth to tenth graders that estimated that approximately 3.7 million youths engage in, and more than 3.2 million are victims of, moderate or serious bullying each year.[5] In 2001, nearly one in five high school students reported that they had thought seriously about killing themselves during the previous twelve months. About one in eleven reported actually attempting suicide.[6]

As they grow up, children will have to learn how to face new fears and new perils we can only imagine. They need guides to help them learn how to navigate dangerous waters, both now and in the future. Now, more than ever before, we seek ways to help our children keep their heads up, their minds clear, and their hearts on fire when danger approaches.

Eight steps to building courage

Raising Courageous Kids describes the development of courage in children in eight steps from infancy to early adolescence. At each step, children experience a *discovery* that enables them to learn an essential *strength*.

- From *power* to *willpower*
- From *community* to *caring*
- From *danger* to *vigilance*
- From *fear* to *composure*
- From *self* to *empathy*
- From *morality* to *integrity*
- From *justice* to *honor*
- From *responsibility* to *valor*

The eight steps are arranged in a *developmental sequence* of critical periods. *Willpower*, for example, makes its first appearance as babies push themselves up from their cribs, reach for objects, and gesture to a parent for help. Learning to *care* is a critical development of early childhood. If children do not learn to care about others by their third birthday, they may lose the capacity to care regardless of the love and devotion showered on them later. Brain pathways necessary for caring that are not activated by that age may remain inactive.

The flow from one step to another is *cyclical*, not linear. The eight steps are more like dance steps than stair steps. They are part of a pattern repeated throughout our lives. For example, although it has its origins in infancy, *willpower* is continuously shaped throughout a person's life. Although *integrity* has its greatest significance during middle childhood, it originates in early childhood.

Movement from one step to another occurs *naturally*. *Raising Courageous Kids* is not a program, curriculum or childrearing script. The parents of Amanda Valance did not announce, "Today, we are going to teach you to do something courageous." Amanda absorbed the lessons of courage by observing her parents, by receiving their gifts of love, and by testing herself as she grew up.

Willpower, caring, vigilance, composure, empathy, integrity, honor, and valor develop through practice, like steel tempered by fire. At some point, an extraordinary challenge will test the resilience of these strengths. During those moments, the eight strengths will combine as links in a ring of valor, each necessary to face life courageously.

As you read the developmental milestones associated with each step (see appendix, pages 213-239), you will discover that many are already part of your childrearing. *Raising Courageous Kids* is more than a celebration of the amazing powers of the human spirit that have already taken place. It is also a celebration of the wonderful things you do to inspire your children to rise above fear and give something worthwhile back to life.

How to use this book

At each of the eight steps, *Raising Courageous Kids* will help you

- appreciate how courage originates and unfolds from birth to fourteen;

- use developmental milestones to observe your children's progress;
- discover how reading and telling stories teach children about courage;
- introduce activities that give your children practice opportunities to develop the strengths that contribute to courage;
- reflect on your personal journey toward courage and heroism; and
- establish a growth-producing relationship that nurtures in your children the eight steps covered in this book.

Establishing and then maintaining a supportive, loving relationship is critical for nurturing courage. Ideas have to be reinforced by commitment. Great accomplishments are achieved by the accumulation of everyday actions. How we react when our children wake up during the night with a terrifying nightmare or come home with a bloody lip after being hit by a bully makes all the difference in how our children's character takes root and flourishes. In the eight steps that follow, you will find a description of forty-six practices that will help your children achieve greatness in their lives.

A Song of Greatness

When I hear the old men
Telling of heroes,
Telling of great deeds
of ancient days,

When I hear them telling,
Then I think within me
I too am one of these.

When I hear the people
Praising the great ones,
Then I know that I too
Shall be esteemed,
I too when my time comes
Shall do mightily.

A Chippewa Indian chant
(Translated by Mary Austin)

Our greatest monuments to those who take risks
and make sacrifices on behalf of others like Amanda
Valance or any of the heroes of September 11 are not
made of stone, steel, and glass. They are not memorial
plaques or dramatic statues found in parks or in front
of county courthouses. The greatest monument is an
enduring shift in the human spirit, a transformation
made possible by the caring of others.

*The gift of courage is a celebration of the power of the
human spirit.* The care we provide from the moment
children enter our lives makes such character possible.
Because of us, our children may say, "I too have
courage" when faced with difficult situations in the
days to come. Every child who finds the courage to
stand up to fear and the heroism to care for others is
truly a gift to humanity. We need heroes in an age that
requires noble deeds.

Step One

From Power
to Willpower

Keywords:
engagement, sensory awareness,
self-affirmation, self-assertion,
aggression, violence

Emphasis:
Persevere toward a worthy goal.

As a grandfather took his young grandson for a walk in the woods near his farm, the little boy saw a cocoon on a small branch. He asked his grandfather about it. The grandfather replied, "It's a cocoon, a home for a caterpillar that is slowly growing into a butterfly. Soon the butterfly will escape and fly away."

Later that day, the boy returned, broke off the branch holding the cocoon, and brought it back to his room in his grandfather's farmhouse. He felt sorry for the butterfly trapped inside and wanted to help—so he took a table knife and opened the cocoon to set the butterfly free.

Of course, he was disappointed with the results. The boy explained what had happened to his grandfather, who replied: "I forgot to tell you something important when we first saw this cocoon. The cocoon provides safety while the butterfly grows stronger.

"When it is strong enough and ready to leave, it has to fight its way out. The new butterfly becomes stronger and stronger as it pushes and struggles. By the time it breaks free, it has the capacity to fly. You wanted to help, but you didn't understand that the butterfly had to work hard to get out of the cocoon to become strong." Together, grandfather and grandson took the remains of the cocoon back to the forest and buried it under the tree.

Children are like maturing butterflies in this way: Both need a safe place that gives them time to gain strength. Someday, children will use that power to set out on their own.

The growth of courage depends on the continuing recognition and use of one's power.[1] *Power* is the capacity to make things happen. *Willpower* is the intentional use of power to reach a goal and is the foundation for the seven strengths that follow. Willpower first appears when infants deliberately reach for an object or gesture to indicate their desires. For example, when she sees her father at the side of her crib, a baby reaches out with her arms. The father reaches down to pick her up and hold her in his arms. The baby learns that her display of yearning achieves results.

Later, the child sits in her mother's lap and reaches for a cookie on the table. She strains and leans, stretching her arm further and further. The mother notices and pushes the food within her daughter's reach. The mother doesn't pick up the cookie and pop it in her daughter's mouth. Instead, she lets her daughter find satisfaction in achieving a goal.

During the preschool years children begin to exercise willpower in their relationships with peers. When my daughter Sarah was three, I took her to the playground because she wanted to learn how to swing. She sat in the swing and struggled to get moving. She twisted and turned, leaned over and back, frantically stuck her legs out and pulled them back. No matter how hard she worked, she couldn't get the swing moving. She fiercely resisted my offer to help. Then two older grade school girls arrived. They pointed at Sarah and giggled in response to her frantic gyrations.

When she noticed their laughter, Sarah climbed down from the swing, approached the two girls and put her hands on her hips. Then she swayed side to side and defiantly stuck out her tongue. She turned abruptly and marched back to the swing to resume her struggle. Eventually her persistence achieved success.

Courage and heroism are based on *free will*. They are choices that emerge from a belief in our power and our capacity to act decisively. Fallon Richards (page 24) felt this *willpower* when she pulled her grandfather from his burning home. She saw the danger and chose to bring him to safety. She believed in her power to achieve a goal.

Mighty Heart
Fallon Richards

On July 6, 1999, twelve-year-old Fallon Richards, motivated by the force of hope, saved her grandfather from a fire. During a visit to his Alabama mobile home, fire broke out in the kitchen, which adjoined his bedroom, and quickly filled the two rooms with dense smoke. When she smelled the smoke, Fallon ran through the burning kitchen to get to her grandfather's bedroom, where he was confined to a hospital bed. She alerted him to the fire, went to the back porch and shouted for help, then returned to her grandfather's side. She grasped him by the legs, pulled him from the bed to the floor, and then dragged him from the bedroom to the back door and outside to the porch. Neighbors arrived and took her grandfather to safety. Fallon, who is asthmatic, was taken to the hospital for treatment of smoke inhalation and a second-degree burn to her arm. She recovered.[2]

Nurturing willpower

- **Encourage children to use their senses**
- **Recognize and support children's self-affirmation**
- **Respond positively to self-assertion**
- **Give children "power moments"**
- **Affirm children's hope in their future**
- **Expect greatness**
- **Explore the proper use of power in conflict**

For children to gain willpower, a caring person has to help connect them to the world around them. Children thrive from experiences of touch, motion, sound, and light that both invite and inspire them to explore and experience what life has to offer.

Some children may never receive such invitations, and life will hold less joy for them than it does for children whose parents provide opportunities for them to explore and test their capabilities. When caring responses to curiosity or need are absent, infants' cries remain unanswered. They come to believe that their actions have no effect on their surroundings. Their expression of willpower dissolves from frustrated cries to rage and finally to silence. Hopelessness makes them withdraw. In the absence of love, power retreats and then vanishes. These children lose the will to live.

If this lack of engagement continues, children may never develop curiosity, hope, or the ability to feel connected to other people and the world around them. Their wellspring of power has gone dry. In contrast, parents who are an integral part of their children's lives nurture willpower and reward initiative.

Encourage children
to use their senses

Several years ago I watched a next-door neighbor walking around his yard with his infant son. He walked slowly, cradling the little boy securely in his arms. Every few steps he stopped at a tree to hold a leaf up to his son's face. Occasionally he crouched, setting the infant on the ground to watch a crawling bug or touch the soft grass. After a few moments, he would gently lift the child back into his arms and continue their journey.

This playful ritual provided an opportunity for the father to share the world with his child. As a three-year-old, the child pushed his own little plastic mower around the yard when his father mowed the lawn. When his father cleaned up after their dog, the young boy walked beside him with his own plastic bucket. The father and child were building a partnership that fostered the boy's willpower and confidence.

Inviting children to use their senses promotes the development of courage in two ways: 1) awareness of our environment is crucial to our sense of compassion and ability to manage risk; and 2) sensory awareness is the basis for empathy. For example, an older child who intervenes when a bully uses racial insults to humiliate a classmate needs to be aware of many things. He first notices what is happening, then feels compassion for the victim, and finally evaluates the right time and approach for his intervention. Or, he may decide not to intervene at all, giving his classmate the opportunity to stand up to the bully on his own.

Recognize and support children's self-affirmation

A child tugged and pulled at a weed while her mother gardened. After considerable effort, the weed popped from the ground, and the little girl fell backward. Waving the plant over her head like a victory baton, the toddler shouted, "Look, Mama, at what I DID!" Her mother replied, "Marie, good job! You really had to work at that!" The child proudly replied, "Yes, Mama, and the WHOLE WORLD had a hold of the other end!"

Self-affirmation, a declaration of self-respect and personal worth, is an expression of willpower. When children affirm themselves, they announce to another person that they bring something positive to life. With self-affirmation, children say, "Hey, I'm somebody!" Self-affirmation is an "I-plus" response to life.

Affirming your child

Gradually turning control over to a child is a critical element in contributing to self-discipline. Full independence from parents at maturity is best achieved one step at a time, beginning during early childhood.

Make a list of all the issues, large and small, that bring you into conflict with your child. Count the number of times you react negatively when one of these issues arises during a typical three-hour block of time that you are with your child.

During the same period, also note how many times you engage your child in a pleasant manner. Write as many examples of your typical positive responses as you can.

Compare the two numbers. Ideally, we should find at least two positives for every single negative. To achieve a more favorable ratio, we can increase the positives, decrease the negatives, or do both. To decrease the negatives, we can deliberately ignore a minor conflict and allow a child to take responsibility for the problem.

Return to the list of conflict issues you created. For each incident, decide whether the problem is something that requires your intervention or whether you can hand its resolution over to your child. For example, let's say you have a long list of negative conflicts. One of them is arguing over the mess in your teenager's room. You might decide that issue is a low priority compared to others. To remove it from your intervention list, you could decide to let your teen decide how his room appears.

The easiest form of self-affirmation for young children is nonverbal. Children point to things, clap their hands, and make sounds to "show off" to their parents. Even though babies cannot say, "Look at what I did!" they can point and clap their hands.

As children learn to speak, the ability to express their ideas and to be heard is a great source of power. Listening to children's stories about the events of their day increases their confidence—another important component of courage.

Respond positively to self-assertion

In a workshop for professionals on how to communicate with toddlers, Francesca Adler-Baeder's daughter assisted her with a demonstration. Dr. Adler-Baeder asked Jessica to demonstrate the "Eensy-Weensy Spider" song and hand movement to the assembled group. The mother joined in as Jessica began to sing. Suddenly Jessica stopped, turned to her mother, waved her hand, and told her firmly, "NO! I do it." She then sang the song alone for a few moments. Turning to one of the participants sitting in a nearby chair, Jessica invited her to participate. "You can sing it!"

Jessica's initial comment, "NO, I do it!" was an example of self-assertion. She chose how, when, and with whom she wanted to share the song. Jessica responded *assertively* to express her power on her own behalf. She also wanted to share her power with a stranger. Her mother gave her that opportunity.

Self-assertion is persistence, an early sign of fortitude that emerges at Step Eight (From Responsibility to Valor). A child falls down and then gets back up. Another child rebuilds a tower of blocks that toppled over. A third child struggles to tie her shoelaces. Self-assertion is a display of persistent will.

Self-assertion can bring children into conflict with others. Infants may express willpower as acts of resistance. They may kick, cry, and scream when thwarted. As they grow older, temper tantrums decline while defiance becomes more focused and organized. At about two years of age, a child may look her parents in the eyes, dig in her heels, and say, "NO!" And even as we respond, "Oh, yes you will!" as we carry her off to bed, we should be cheering inside. We have a child with spunk and grit, one unafraid to speak up and oppose an obstacle. Even though being the object of that opposition is uncomfortable, loving parents provide opportunities for children to practice self-assertion. Our task is to guide and shape their will, not to break it.

Like athletes in vigorous training, healthy children need to exert will to become stronger. Saying "NO!" is part of that mental flexing. Strong and reasonably assertive responses by parents will begin to establish fair borders around the child's power. Parents who consistently yield to children's assertiveness create tyrants. Parents who suppress children's assertiveness create victims. Parents who gradually *share* power and who respect assertiveness in their children contribute to their healthy expression of power and self-control.

The "NO!" that we found frustrating when the child was young gains dramatic significance when the child is fourteen and approached by a peer offering a marijuana joint. "No," our teenager tells the person. "I'm not interested." The origins of this fortitude, this resistance to pressure and the exercise of free will originates in the child's practice of assertiveness as a toddler. Strip children of power at a young age, and we make them vulnerable to destructive manipulation later in life. Grit, gumption, and self-assertion are critical responses to destructive peer pressure.

I agree with Thoreau's observation that "the most alive is the wildest." In *Where the Wild Things Are* by Maurice Sendak (Harper and Row, 1963) there is a pivotal moment in the story when young Max is threatened by the "wild things" of the jungle. Instead of running away, Max faces his tormentors and commands them to "BE STILL." Then Max tames them ". . . with a magic trick of staring into their yellow eyes without blinking once and they were all frightened and called him the most wild thing of all. . . ." Children love the book because Max tells them that they can find the power to control their fears.[3]

Give children "power moments"

As a preschool teacher at Bowling Green State University, I once wore a blindfold for an entire morning to challenge children to think about sensory disabilities. While I sat listening to the buzz of activity around me, two four-year-olds in my group approached, dropped to their hands and knees, and volunteered to be my "guide dogs." I toured the classroom on my knees, holding their belts as we scooted from one area to another.

Exploring our sensory world
(all ages)

Our first experiences as infants were explorations of our surrounding sensory world. As we grow older, familiarity may cause us to become less aware of the sensory experience. We tend to supplement real experience with predefined notions about something based on our empirical experiences.

Invite your child to play an exploring game with you. Give him a paper bag and ask him to place interesting objects from around the house in the bag. These objects should be safe and pleasant to touch. Ask him to keep the names of the objects a secret. When he returns with the objects in his paper sack, reach inside to hold and touch what he found for you.

You will experience a natural inclination to name what is there. Resist that impulse and focus on how the object actually feels. If a child brings you an orange, for example, avoid saying, "Oh, that's an orange." Of course, the word will come to mind, but focus on experiencing the orange as an object with its own uniqueness. Your goal is to explore the object's textures without actually seeing or evaluating what you are touching.

Experience the orange in such a way that you could pick it out of a basket of several other oranges. Repeat with other found objects. Ask your child if he would like to have a turn after you find objects for him to touch. When he reaches inside the bag, emphasize touching the object without having to name it.[4]

When the group went outside to play later that morning, I decided to remain behind in the classroom for a while. Susan, a shy and cautious child, asked me if she could take me outside. I cautiously agreed, pleased to see evidence of her courage and kindness. We left the building, and she led me into an open area. "Wait here," she said as she let go of my hand. So, I stood there, awkwardly alone and blindfolded, certain that the university president would pass by and wonder why one of his faculty was behaving so strangely.

When Susan returned, her slender fingers squeezed a small bouquet of wildflowers into my hand. "These are for you," she said. Our relationship would never be the same. She had recognized her power and her ability to use it positively.

Susan was not afraid of me when I was handicapped. Instead of retreating from my "strength," she approached my "weakness" with kindness. The power gap between us had diminished, and she felt more comfortable reaching out to me.

Parents and teachers contribute to children's ability to act with purpose by asking them for help even when the help is not actually needed. A father who is carrying a couple of bags of groceries, for example, might ask his preschooler to open a door for him. Even though he could manage on his own, he gives his child an opportunity to feel masterful. Similarly, he asks the packer at the grocery store to fill a small bag for his child to carry. Afterward, the father thanks his child for helping him and expresses admiration for his growing capabilities. Children who feel respected and encouraged by their parents are more likely to provide help later when their help could make a more significant contribution. Taking the time when children are young to nurture willpower and purpose is an investment that builds responsibility.

Affirm children's hope in their future

My first childhood friend was a dreamer. Bobby moved in down the street from my Detroit home when

I was about seven years old. He shared his hopes with me one afternoon while we sat on a curb and threw stones into a gravel street. More than anything else in the world my friend wanted to own a ranch and raise horses when he grew up. "How about you?" he asked. Would I like to join him? This was no idle boast to pass the time on a lazy summer afternoon. No, this was serious stuff, a promise Bobby made to himself, but one he wanted to share with a friend. He described his dream with warmth and enthusiasm.

Me too, I thought. Maybe I could have a ranch right next to his. This was a bold vision for a child with severe asthma. There were nights when I thought I would not have a future. Bobby's vision, however, was contagious. As I listened to him, I began to imagine living where there were gentle rolling hills, lush woods, and a ranch better than what we saw on television on *Gunsmoke* or *Bonanza*. This place was far from the urban streets where we lived. The future— what wonderful opportunities it held for us during those warm summer days! We looked forward to a tomorrow that beckoned with the promise of success and happiness. As Carl Sandburg wrote, "Nothing happens unless first a dream."

The great American fairy tale *The Wizard of Oz* is based on hope. Although they have different goals, Dorothy, the Tin Man, the Scarecrow, and the Lion follow the Yellow Brick Road because of their hope for success. Each pursues a different vision while bound together in hope.

Hope is a wellspring of courage and heroism. The ability to envision and hope for a positive outcome is a powerful catalyst in the midst of difficult circumstances. Amanda Valance had hope in the moment between the alligator's attack and pulling her friend from the canal. Fallon Richards certainly felt hope too that her grandfather would make it out safe when she pulled him from his burning mobile home. Hope energized them.

When my son Bill was about eight years old, I once drove him to school while in a melancholy mood. I told him I was feeling sad and quiet. I wanted him to know that this gloom was mine alone and that he had no responsibility for how I felt. Bill listened carefully, then looked at me seriously and reached across the front seat. He patted my leg gently and said in a clear, firm voice, "Dad, you just got to have hope."

This was Bill's way of reaching out to me in a vulnerable moment. With one simple comment, he lifted my spirit and brought a smile to my face. Bill lived up to Kahlil Gibran's words, "He alone is great who turns the voice of the wind into a song made sweeter by his own loving."

The presence of hope during childhood is evidence of *resiliency*, the ability to rebound after loss and disappointment. Resilient children respond to hard times, such as a death in the family, violence in school, or personal disappointment, with faith in their power to overcome. They believe that if they keep working and keep trying, success will follow. Children who do not have such hope when faced with life challenges are more vulnerable and more likely to suffer from depression, take drugs, or act out in some unhealthy manner.

Expect greatness

Young people need adults in their lives who provide a strong compass and expect greatness. In 2002, National Public Radio's Juan Williams talked to seven students who were about to be the first African-American women to graduate from the Citadel, a prestigious military school in Charleston, South Carolina.[5] Many of these students were drawn to older African-American women who worked as nonprofessional staff at the institution. These mature adults provided support and encouragement to the young women who were struggling to be successful in an environment dominated by white men.

During the NPR interview, a student described an encounter with one of these women. Although close to graduation, the student was discouraged and ready to quit. She told her mentor, "I can't do this!" The older woman responded immediately and firmly. "Yes, you *will* do this." The student could literally feel the "push" of the other woman, pressing her at a vulnerable moment when such firmness was exactly what she needed.

The older woman did not say, "You *can* do this," or "You *could* do this," or even "You *might* do this." She said, "You *will* do this." There was no waffling, wavering, or uncertainty in her response of *willpower*. The older woman was decisive, moved by her confidence in the abilities of the younger woman.

The young woman wanted to stay but felt weak and frightened by the possibility of failure. Here was a *pivotal moment*: A point in time when a decision would be made that had powerful implications for the future.

At this moment, the mentor's firmness became a borrowed strength that reenergized the young woman. Anything less than firmness may have failed her. The student would go on to graduate with pride.

Children need to witness the confidence their parents and other adults have for them. They need champions who will stand up for their beliefs and expect greatness from them. Greatness does not mean perfection or even success. Greatness means reaching for something important. Whether it is a young child discouraged about completing a class project or a young adult ready to give up and quit school, our loving expectations and confidence may be what is necessary to carry them through. Reaching for greatness is a demonstration of power. Willpower is necessary for achieving success.

Explore the proper use of power in conflict

Assertion means being firm about what we want or do not want. *Aggression* is direct intervention to control another person's behavior. Aggression creates an opposition of wills. Is aggression bad? Sometimes. A child might grab a toy from another child and push him down. Unreasonable and harmful aggression carried out for selfish purposes is predatory. Predatory aggression destroys relationships and invites counter-aggression. However, some forms of aggression are prosocial. For example, a child may protect her sister by pushing her out of harm's way. Another child may physically intervene when a bully begins beating a helpless classmate. In both cases, children use force as a tool for caring.

Parents often have to be aggressive in order to protect their children. Sometimes parents intervene strongly to ensure their children learn reasonable limits. However, nonviolent, prosocial aggression may be necessary when assertion is insufficient. When a father tells his three-year-old, "Mary, please stay in the yard. The street is a dangerous place to play," he makes an *assertion*. Mary forgets or decides to challenge his limit and walks out into the street. If the father physically leads her back to the yard against her will, his prosocial *aggression* keeps her safe.

Consider Jacob Russell Ryker's (see page 39) response to the gunman in his high school cafeteria. Even though wounded, Jacob found the power to rise from the floor and to use force to stop the attack. His timely aggression saved lives.

Children who occasionally defend objects in their possession or even take toys from their peers are particularly likely to help and share spontaneously at other times. On the other hand, children who are *frequently* aggressive rarely show kindness, if at all. Apparently, a certain level of dominance and assertiveness may be necessary for children to offer help spontaneously. These children have learned to be selective in the use of force and not to withdraw in difficult circumstances.[6]

Violence is the last resort for gaining power. A child whose positive attempts to achieve success fail may grasp for control by lashing out. The violent individual tries to accomplish a goal by *hurting* someone. Violence is a desperate act, the result of feeling power*less*, not power*ful*.

Mighty Heart
Jacob Russell Ryker

On May 21, 1998, seventeen-year-old Jacob Ryker did not hesitate to use force to save the lives of his Springfield, Oregon, classmates. A fifteen-year-old boy entered a crowded high school cafeteria and opened fire with a semiautomatic rifle. One student in the cafeteria was killed and twenty-five were wounded. Jacob was thrown to the floor by a gunshot to the chest. When the gunman stopped to reload his weapon, Jacob rose and, despite his severe wound, charged the shooter, who fell to the floor and lost his weapon. As several other students rose from the floor to help Jacob, the shooter managed to reveal a handgun, which Jacob grabbed. The weapon fired, further wounding Jacob in the hand. Police arrived and arrested the attacker. Jacob survived the attack, and his heroism saved numerous lives.[7]

Can *violence* be prosocial? While nonviolence should be our primary goal in resolving conflict, the absolute, universal application of nonviolence is troubling. Is violence always wrong? Are some things worth a fight? If a mother was carjacked with her toddler in the back seat, would you want her to (a) engage her attackers in a discussion of the moral implications of their action; (b) do nothing at all; or (c) fight back? Does it matter that a child is involved? Does the mother's goal of protecting her child justify the use of violence? If she fights back with all the fury she can muster her purpose is to defend her child. This is a desperate fight not of her choosing.

Passive onlookers contribute to predatory violence. The teenage shooters at Columbine High School were mercilessly teased and humiliated by their classmates. Did other students intervene to stop the ridicule? Did they go to their teachers and demand they intervene? If the students at Columbine had learned the value of intervention on behalf of others, they might have prevented the isolation and explosive outrage of two of their classmates.

If we encourage children to stand up to predators when adult help is not available, then we have to prepare them to respond directly to the threat of violence. This does not mean that we should tell our children to intervene in every schoolyard fight they see—but it *does* mean that we encourage them to work either alone or with others to break patterns of victimization and bullying when they are encountered. One way to break these patterns is to come to the defense of the victim. Another is to remove the emotional reward of the bully by calling his bluff—an action that only the victim can take. The following incident provides an example of this challenge.

When I was fourteen years old, a bully beat me up. Five friends and I were playing a pickup game of baseball one evening on a school playground near my Detroit home. A seventeen-year-old stranger who was walking by accused me of making an obscene gesture at his girlfriend. He probably picked me out of the group because I was the tallest, and he wanted to show off in front of his girlfriend. He walked over and began pushing me. He was not bluffing. I resisted and we began to fight.

Unfortunately, I was not much of a street fighter. He quickly launched a few strong blows to my face and wrestled me to the ground, then pinned my arms with his knees and began smashing my face with his fists. I began to lose consciousness and was helpless as he continued to beat me. None of my friends did anything to stop him.

I can understand why they held back at first. It was not their weakness or fear that made them stand back, but a primitive pack curiosity about dominance and power. There is something very "red of tooth and claw" about schoolyard fights. They wanted to see how I did on my own, presumably to determine my social fitness to be part of the group. They wanted to see how I fulfilled my responsibility to fight for myself (and lose, if it came to that).

Children should not grow up thinking that someone else will always come to their rescue. Sometimes we have to rescue ourselves, or at the least fail trying. In some circumstances we stand and fight alone. That's the way of the world. Research on bullying shows that frequently victimized children often reinforce their attackers by giving in to their demands. Victims cry, assume defensive postures, and fail to fight back. They radiate anxious vulnerability.[8]

Powerlessness produces victims who embolden predators. Parents and teachers should encourage children to demonstrate resilience and integrity when bullied, rather than fear and helplessness. Many martial arts schools offer self-defense courses for children. The strict discipline of these schools can be a useful and healthy learning experience for children. Parents should first attend as observers to evaluate the suitability of the environment and the instructor's style for their child. Schools that encourage a highly competitive "red of tooth and claw" approach tend to polarize all people into bullies and victims. In contrast, the best schools do not to turn victims into bullies, but instead rob bullies of their potential victims.

Courage means using power to defend oneself when necessary. Courage also means intervening to stop brutality of the defenseless. Instead of fleeing, I stood up for myself. Would my friends have stood idly by until I was beaten to death? This was a playground, not the Roman Colosseum. I was an innocent victim, not a gladiator. My attacker did not want to simply win a contest of power. He wanted the blood of a badly defeated stranger on his hands. Such displays of malevolence have little to do with the heated test of wills that each of us has seen and experienced while we were growing up.

Every child, every person, has a choice: To respond as a victim trembling in a corner, or to gallantly face adversity with hope, strength, and determination. Parents provide encouragement, support, and a place for children to find recuperation and renewal. Children will soon emerge from their cocoons not as fragile butterflies but as individuals with decisive power. Ultimately, they can become their own champions in the march to valor.

Step Two

From Community to Caring

Keywords:
connection, outsider, devotion,
love, rapport, stranger

Emphasis:
Love your neighbor as yourself.

During the 1980s, high interest rates and operating costs placed a great burden on farming communities across the nation. Faced with reduced land values, many Kansas families lost their farms. Families moved to the city, and the next generation of young people turned away from farming. A group of men from southeast Kansas, alarmed by the loss of population in their small rural community, paid an unannounced visit to Kansas State University to seek help. Administrators scrambled to find faculty who could meet with them to discuss the problems facing their community. I was one of the people chosen to meet with the farmers. I asked the group if their community was pulling together to face the crisis.

Rudy, a seventy-year-old man with short-cropped white hair and a ruddy, wind-creased face, raised his hand. Then his face sagged and his eyes brimmed with tears. "This reminds me of a sad time from my childhood, a sad time. All these years . . . but I can't forget."

When Rudy was about fourteen years old, the elderly widower who lived on the farm adjacent to his family property accidentally killed a four-year-old girl when he backed his car out of a parking place in town. He had not seen the child. The tragedy filled the community with grief.

One afternoon, shortly after the child's funeral, Rudy was walking to town on the gravel road that passed by the widower's farm. As he approached his neighbor's property, Rudy could see the elderly man walking down his driveway to his mailbox. They met there, separated by a fence.

"The old man looked at me and I stopped. His eyes filled with tears. Then he began talking as tears streamed down his face: 'I didn't see her; I didn't know she was there! Oh, I am so sorry! Why didn't God take me, not her?'"

"I wanted so much to get close to him, to put my arms around him and tell him that it would be all right, that my family and I still cared about him. But I didn't.

I was too scared. I just couldn't bring myself to get over that fence to give him a hug. After he talked for a bit, my neighbor turned and slowly hobbled back to his home, head down and back bent by the burden of the heartbreak. Since that day I've regretted not jumping the fence to show that old man that I cared about him."

As he shared his memory, Rudy kneaded his hands together, big hands callused from hard work. He was working hard now to stay in control of his emotions. When he finished talking, a heavy silence filled the room. His neighbors seated around the long mahogany table sat motionless, gazing into their folded hands as though they were crystal balls.

What can we say to soothe a decades-old hurt?

I responded, "A missed opportunity? Perhaps. Even so, Rudy, you took action. You *stopped*. Others may have passed him by. You didn't. You stopped and listened to him. For just a few moments, he had the opportunity to tell a young neighbor his story of overwhelming grief and regret. At a critical moment, you became his witness. That night, when he put his head down on his pillow, he may have slept just a little more deeply because he knew you listened and would remember his story. You witnessed and recorded the pain he felt. Rudy, your display of devotion showed him that he was no longer alone."

The word "wretched" comes from the Middle English *wrecche*, for exile, a person without kin nearby, isolated from love, and dehumanized by circumstances. What a wretched experience it is, to be exiled from family and friends. What pain could be greater than to stand outside of the human community?

Caring: Drawing the circles together

Among the tribes of Northern Natal in sub-Saharan Africa, one person greets another with *"Sawu bona,"* meaning, "I see you." The other replies, *"Sikhona,"* "I am here." This exchange reflects the spirit of *Ubuntu,* which holds that "a person is not a person until seen by other people." Our lives must be recognized by a community to be real.

We all need some participation in community, even if we prefer solitude to crowds. With no one to talk to, how can we think through our problems, find reassurance when we feel like giving up, or make discoveries about what we cherish? No wonder studies show that children would rather be punished than be ignored. To be "not seen" is a *wretched* experience.

The need for connection is never more urgent than when someone is threatened. This is a moment of vulnerability that may be elevated to terror when one is alone. In desperate conditions, survival may depend on the willingness of others to take risks or make sacrifices on another's behalf.

A young stranger with a red bandana around his head emerged from the clouds of dust and debris on the seventy-fifth floor of the World Trade Center to repeatedly guide trapped office workers to safety; his parents later identified him as their son, Welles Crowther, from the descriptions provided by those he saved. Welles, a volunteer firefighter, died after returning to find more of his office colleagues.

What drives heroic hearts to face danger in order to protect others? Why did fifteen-year-old Jacob Ryker rise from the cafeteria floor after being shot in the chest to tackle the shooter? Or Fallon Richards fight her way through the flames in her grandfather's home? They found the power to act because they cared about someone other than themselves. Jacob had to stop the killing of his classmates. Fallon risked her life out of love for her grandfather.

Imagine every person who has been part of your life as a circle intersecting with a central circle, which is your own. The Stoic philosopher Hierocles (c. 1 A.D.) wrote about how thriving communities depend on everyone drawing the surrounding circles of others toward their center.[1] As the "outsider" circles move closer to our center, they begin to touch and overlap with our circle of self. Where there is overlap, the other person becomes an important part of our lives.

The circles of life in our first relationships consist of family members, followed by other relatives and neighbors. Then other circles of life begin to take shape—different sizes, ages, and colors—each approaching our circle as a stranger.

The more its citizens pull these circles toward their own, the stronger the links that give energy and life to communities. An elderly black man living in the mid-South told Clarissa Pinkola Estes a story of African kings called "One Stick, Two Stick."[2]

"And it is the way," he whispered to her, of the old African Kings. A dying old man hands a sturdy stick to his assembled family and neighbors. He asks each of them to break it. All do so easily, even the smallest child. "This is how it is when a soul is alone without anyone. They can be easily broken," he tells them.

Then the man provides those gathered before him with bundles of the sticks. Even the strongest person cannot break the combined sticks. "We are strong when we stand with another soul," he says. "When we are with another, we cannot be broken." Courage and caring teach children to "stand with other souls" and bring vitality to their communities as they grow up.

Nurturing caring

- **Take time to do things with our children**
- **Say "I love you" to our children**
- **Give children at least one affirmation a day**
- **Talk positively with children about their pasts**
- **Expand children's circle of caring**

Caring about others does not spring up unbidden from children's hearts. Children grow up learning to care for others and find community with them by experiencing for themselves the devotion of others. Most importantly, when they were very young, at least one person loved them, nurtured them, and showered them with true devotion.

True devotion is a treasured resource necessary for children to thrive. Loving children involves four gifts that provide the foundation for caring:

- First, we make a *lifetime commitment*. This love endures no matter what.

- Second, we make *all sacrifices* necessary for our children's health and well-being without expectation of return.

- Third, we assume *full responsibility* for our children's welfare and upbringing. We accept the social contract associated with being a parent. We stand with them in times of trouble.

- Finally, we foster a *rapport* with our children that enables us to feel their joy and pain, sadness and fear, anger and serenity.

A pediatric hospital provides many opportunities to witness such devotion. In the long-term-care ward of the hospital where I worked as a play therapist we had a seven-year-old boy whose illness a year earlier left him severely brain damaged. The doctors said that he was in a vegetative state, with little awareness of the world around him and no ability to react to any stimulation except in the most primitive way. Months before I arrived, his parents had stopped visiting him, unable to bear the enormity of their loss.

The little boy was not alone, though. His grandmother visited him every day. She would talk to him, stroke his sandy brown hair, and caress his freckled cheeks. She helped to exercise his legs. Most of the time she simply sat in a chair next to his bed with her arm resting by his side, as though waiting for him to sit up and tell her he was ready to go home.

Sometimes I would visit him when he was alone. I talked to him and stroked his cheek. There were moments when I thought he reacted. Did I see a faint trace of a smile or hear a subtle sound that he could not shape into words? The boy's grandmother had taught me about the power of love to suspend judgment. She was not willing to give up. The grandmother's love not only sustained the boy, it made her believe that she could still nurture her grandson. Even if wrong, she ennobled herself in the choice and inspired hospital workers who witnessed her devotion.

Stanley Greenspan believes that the invitation to love during infancy is a critical experience for

Mighty Heart
Keith Louis Putnam

On August 6, 1998, Keith Louis Putnam was a passenger in a car passing through Hanahan, South Carolina, late at night. He and the driver pulled over when they saw a car stuck at a railroad track at a nearby crossing. They could see a train approaching in the distance, traveling at what was later determined to be about 45 mph. Keith immediately rushed to the stalled vehicle. There he found a twenty-one-year-old woman, unconscious in the driver's seat. Keith pulled her from the car and dragged her out of harm's way. Despite the train bearing down on the car, Keith returned, possibly to make sure no one had been left behind. Too late. The train struck the car, which struck and killed him. Keith was fourteen years old.[6]

intellectual and emotional growth. "Without some degree of this ecstatic wooing by at least one adult who adores her, a child may never know the powerful intoxication of human closeness, never abandon herself to the magnetic pull of human relationships, never see other people as full human beings like herself, capable of feeling what she feels."[3]

This "magnetic pull" is also critical for heroism, as demonstrated by research findings on those who risked their lives to rescue Jews during World War II. These rescuers reported that they grew up in families who were close. Most had a sense of belonging in their communities.[4] In the same way, dedicated civil rights workers from the 1960s have reported warm, cordial, and respecting relationships with parents who demonstrated concern for others.[5]

Love received is passed on to others. Keith Putnam (see page 52) had no idea who was in the vehicle stalled on the railroad tracks. He did not know if the color of the stranger's skin was yellow, black, red, white, or brown. He didn't know the age, sex, or hometown of the person in the car. He knew only that someone was in grave danger. He had to try to help. As he raced alone across the darkened street, he had one goal: if someone is in that car, I have to get them out.

Taking a risk or making a sacrifice for another does not imply indifference toward one's own welfare. On the contrary, caring about others in a mature fashion is an *extension* of caring for oneself. The power that moved Keith and gave him the ability to pull the woman from the vehicle came from all the love the young man experienced throughout his life. The love he had for himself made the person in the car a precious human being, someone who deserved help. Albert Schweitzer wrote, "The fundamental fact of human existence is this: I am a life that wants to live in the midst of other life that wants to live. A thinking man feels compelled to approach all life with the same reverence he has for his own." Keith did not choose death that night. He chose to overcome fear. He chose courage. He chose life.

Take time to do things with our children

One of the most powerful acts of devotion we can offer children is to simply spend time with them. Babies should spend at least half of their waking hours interacting with their parents.[7] We can either invite children to participate in our world (teaching and demonstrating) or take time to participate in their world (playing, learning *with* them).

Six rules for being a good play partner

1. Observe and learn. Why does your child find the play so engaging?

2. Begin by playing on your own but similarly (in parallel) to what your child is doing.

3. Relax and have fun; be childlike but not childish.

4. Always let your child be in control.

5. Gradually introduce new ideas during play that introduce a fun challenge for your child.

6. Maintain harmony by adjusting to your child's shifting mood and purpose.

Inviting a child to share our experience involves making space for them in our daily lives. This is more than just keeping them nearby. We might, for example, share a common hobby with our children, take them to movies we both enjoy, and ask for their cooperation as we work on household tasks.

By entering the world of children we can rediscover our capacity for wonder and simple delight. For many parents, making the adjustments to a child's world is more challenging than making space for them in their adult lives. When we play with children, we have to reinvigorate our childlike self and let them take the lead. We leave the world of adult authority and control behind for a short time.

During a workshop on the special nature of grandparent-child relationships, a great-grandmother told me about a recent visit her seven-year-old granddaughter made to her home. They spent the entire afternoon putting on hats, playing dress-up and having tea parties. When the child left to walk home, she stopped at the front door and turned to her exhausted grandmother. "Oh Gramma, I had so much fun!" "I did too," the grandmother replied, "I'm so glad you could visit!" The child responded breathlessly, "Yeah, Gramma, and there were NO grownups around!"

What makes this experience memorable for children is shared enjoyment. The young girl having a tea party with her grandmother certainly enjoys the fancy hats and china in the table setting. Treating oneself to tea on one's best china is a pleasant self-affirmation, though not as special as being so treated by a grandmother. Long after this young girl grows to adulthood, she will remember that afternoon. *Sawu bona. Sikhona.*

Say "I love you" to our children

The word "love" can have two different meanings. As a *noun*, "love" expresses a feeling of profound connection to another person. Making a clear statement to children of the devotion we feel for them is important. Love can also be used as a *verb* that describes what we do for another. Saying "I love you" can be a statement of what we *do*, not just how we *feel*. Love as a verb carries an obligation of action.

Throughout my childhood my mother told me many times, "Your stepfather really does love you." If true, his love was so distant and abstract that it was meaningless for me. What I needed was a love that hugged me, read to me, took me places, and talked to me, heart-to-heart. Children thrive on verbs, not nouns.

I'll Always Love You, written and illustrated by Hans Wilhelm (Crown, 1985) shows the power of love as both an emotion and an action. As the years go by and a young boy grows older and taller, his beloved Elfie, the best dog in the whole world, grows rounder and rounder. It eventually becomes too difficult for Elfie to climb the stairs. Then one night Elfie dies peacefully in

Mighty Heart
Alana Franklin

On June 1, 1998, Alana Franklin, eleven years old, was visiting her grandmother, her sister, and other relatives including her six-year-old nephew in Silver Springs, Florida. A gunman broke into the first-floor apartment and shot the nephew's mother and two other relatives. When the assailant pursued the mother into the bedroom, Alana and the grandmother fled to summon help.

Alana then returned to the apartment alone, knowing that the six-year-old was in his first-floor bedroom and in immediate danger. She stood in the alley outside the window to his room. She broke and unlocked the window, opened it, and brushed the blinds aside. She saw her young nephew on a bed within reach of the window and the gunman in the doorway. Alana partially entered the room through the window, and pulled the boy outside.

The assailant then realized that they were escaping, and fired from the window as Alana carried her nephew to safety, narrowly missing both children. Police arrived, and arrested the man after a four-hour standoff. Alana and her nephew were safe.[8]

her sleep. The boy's grief is soothed by his memories. "We buried Elfie together. We all cried and hugged each other. My brother and sister loved Elfie a lot, but they never told her so. I was very sad too, but it helped to remember that I had told her every night, 'I'll always love you.'"

The boy's tears are more than an expression of mourning; they are a celebration of his love displayed in word and action for his lifelong companion. The memories of that love will help him survive his grief. The boy's story shows us the importance of loving when we have the opportunity.

Heroism is certainly an act of love. Alana Franklin (page 57) put Saint Augustine's words, "If you love me, let it appear," into action when she returned to rescue her nephew.

Give children at least one affirmation a day

For several years I served as director of the Child Development Center at Texas Tech University. Beverly Vinson, a teacher who worked with three-year-olds, employed a delightful strategy for dismissing children individually to the restroom after a group activity. She would look directly at each child, and make a clear and sincere affirmation of appreciation to that child. She might say, "Jamie, I really appreciate the warm smile you gave me this morning. That started my day just right!" Then Jamie would leave to wash his hands. Then she would address the next child, "Sarah, I really appreciated your kindness this morning. Maria was crying and you gave her your doll."

The Treasure Chest
(all ages)

Collect items that provide a historical record of your child's life as he or she outgrows them. Examples include a painting, a clay figurine the child made, a tattered doll, a toy, a comic book, a baseball, a tie, a pair of shoes, a piece of homework with a teacher's comment. Imagine your child as an adult. Would seeing these items bring your adult child, and possibly your grandchildren, pleasure?

Place the items in a large plastic storage box with a secure lid. Write your child's name permanently in a prominent location. You could also include a journal that lists the objects, the date, and their significance. Keep the box in a safe place within easy access.

To keep such treasures is a clear demonstration of love and respect. This Treasure Chest can be useful in three ways. First, it can be quickly taken to a place of safety in the event of fire or natural disaster. Although these items have no real monetary value, their importance to a grownup child can be enormous. Second, you could get the chest out on the child's birthday and talk about some of the items as a way to share memories. Third, when your child grows up, the items in the chest will bring back fond memories. You can talk about the items with your grandchildren if you should have them. At some point, you can permanently pass on the Treasure Chest to your adult child.

There were fourteen children in her class. During her comments, children sat in rapt attention, not a word spoken. She treated all children equally and made sure all of her observations were meaningful and clear.

The best affirmations are *specific* ("You cleaned up the water you spilled") instead of vague ("You sure were nice"). They identify *consequences* ("What you did really helps me") instead of personal qualities ("You are such a good boy"). Specific affirmations that emphasize positive consequences have the power to teach and strengthen behavior.

Just a few words can have powerful implications for a child. A junior high teacher in one of my workshops raised her hand when we talked about children's need for affirmation. In a tearful voice, she told the group that her life was changed for the better by the affirmation and encouragement written by a teacher in her high school yearbook. She traced her choice of career back to that moment. Her memory is a testimony to the transforming power of affirmation.

Another teacher recalled being pushed through a cold hospital hallway on her way to surgery. As she waited to be brought into the operating room, a nurse who accompanied her gently touched her shoulder, bent closely to her face, and then whispered words of affirmation and encouragement in her ear. The nurse's words brought her peace and hope.

Talk positively with children about their pasts

The story of a child's birth can be one of the most powerful stories in a child's life. As children's concepts of time begin to take shape, they first turn their attention to the past. The past anchors children's lives while the future beckons with possibilities. Having no memory of their first days, children need to hear the story of their beginning from those who were present. In *Knots on a Counting Rope* by Bill Martin and John Archambault (Henry Holt, 1987), a young boy and his grandfather sit together around a campfire. The boy asks,

Tell me the story once again, Grandfather. Tell me who I am.

I have told you many times, Boy. You know the story by heart.

But it sounds better when you tell it, Grandfather.

Then listen very carefully. This may be the last telling.

Grandfather then tells his grandson about the night of his birth, and the fear, excitement, and love that his family felt as he made his dramatic entry into the world. But he was weak and close to death. Then an omen foretold of the resilience he would find to live. The boy would need to find this courage, for he was born blind.

All children will have to cross their dark mountains someday. The stories of their births can remind children of the love and sacrifice that brought them into the world and nurtured them as they grew. The story of their birth describes the origins of their nobility.

The day you were born
(all ages)

The story of one's birth can be one of the most powerful narratives in a person's life. Have you talked about this experience with your children? Describe the events surrounding your children's births. Arrange the events along a timeline that begins before labor and ends with your children safe and secure at home. If you adopted your children, "birth" begins on the day you brought the child home. If you are a stepparent, talk about the first day you met. Describe the experience in words your children can understand. Invite children to ask questions. Be honest but avoid misinformation. The idea is to convey to your children the excitement, concern, hard work, and joy surrounding their entry into your life.

Expand children's circle of caring

While waiting in line at the grocery store, a toddler gazes at me from the safety of his mother's arms. He smiles. I return his smile. The child then holds out his tattered teddy bear to me. My smile widens and I nod to him. Mother notices the exchange. She smiles at me and then looks at her son. "You like Benny-bear, don't you." As his mother walks away, he leans over her shoulder to maintain eye contact with me. Our eyes meet for a moment and then he's gone from view.

From a safe and respectful distance, I wanted my actions to send the child a message: "Even people you do not know care about you. I am part of your community."

In their research on heroism, Samuel and Pearl Oliner invented the dimension of "extensivity"—the extent to which caring goes, how far it reaches out to include outsiders and not just to the intimates in our own group. Extensivity also relates to how strongly we feel that justice is not only for ourselves and our own kind, but for others beyond our group. The Oliners believed that extensivity is the essence of the altruistic personality, a person who shows caring without concern for personal gain.[9]

Emphasizing the unity and sacredness of all life is an important element in many spiritual teachings, especially among Native Americans. The Lakota Sioux look toward Father Sky and declare: "*Mitakuye oyasin*"—"We are all one people."[10] One way we put this idea into practice is by encouraging children to volunteer community service.

Sixteen-year-old Stefania Podgorska, a resident of Przemyl, Poland, during World War II, was deeply affected by the cruelty toward Jews she witnessed. She described an incident that contributed to her moral conviction that led to her becoming a heroic rescuer:

A Jewish boy, maybe ten years of age, was walking down the street. Another boy, who was not Jewish, started to yell a little at this Jewish boy. And so an ordinary worker, maybe thirty, asked the non-Jewish boy, "Why do you yell at him?" And this boy said, "Well, because he is a Jew." And this man said, "So what he's a Jew?

Look at him. He is the same as you. You see he is not different. Just the Germans made the difference. . . . Look at him—the same skin as yours, as mine, like everyone. . . . You have to be friendly. There is a war now, and when the war finishes we will all again be friendly." And the man told the boys to shake hands and be friends.

For me, this was something new. And you'll laugh when I say this, but when I came home, I looked at my skin. You see I looked, and I said [to myself], "Of course we are the same!"[11]

This example of care is remarkable, not only because it reveals the teenager's identification with the victim, but also the intervention of a neighbor in the cruelty of war, a profoundly risky act at that time.

Six rules for being a kind stranger

1. Be friendly from a reasonable distance.

2. Recognize and be friendly to the child's parent.

3. Never touch the child without the parent's permission.

4. If you want to give the child something, give it to the parent or ask the parent for permission.

5. Be supportive of parents who are having a difficult time with a child.

6. Speak positively about the child to the parent if you have the opportunity.

Pitarim Sorokin used the term "tribal altruism" to refer to the consequence of isolating children from those they do not know and creating suspicion of outsiders.[12] Unlike positive altruism, *tribal* altruism emphasizes being kind and caring only within a restricted, familiar group. Tribal altruists view those who belong to the familiar group as more important than outsiders. Tribal altruism is associated with the "Balkanization" of America, the fragmentation of citizens into smaller cultural and ethnic groups that insulate themselves from the suffering of those in other groups. It is the driving force behind racial conflict, religious intolerance, and war.

When we teach children to be afraid of strangers we risk converting them into tribal altruists. Of course, we should teach them to be vigilant (see Step Three, "From Danger to Vigilance"). But fearing strangers shrinks children's circles of caring. Self-confidence is eroded by mistrust that weakens the community.

Strangers can express devotion through small acts of kindness. While driving to work one morning during the worst days of the Serbian-Albanian conflict in the former Yugoslavia, I heard an Albanian refugee living in Chicago talking on the radio about his first months living in America. He became emotional when he talked about his young daughter on her way to first- grade class. When the child rushed home later that day, she breathlessly told her father about her amazing experience. The father reported that his daughter could barely restrain her enthusiasm. "And father, the policeman *caressed* my cheek. He *caressed* my cheek." As the father described his conversation with the reporter, he put emphasis on the word "caress."

Would you care?
(elementary)

Ask your child to reflect on and assess his or her caring. Create several opportunities, some requiring courage and others more neutral (or use the list below) and ask your child, Would you care if . . .

- you saw someone deliberately hurting a dog?

- you saw someone laughing when someone tells a funny joke?

- you saw a classmate put a pill in a teacher's coffee cup when she was not looking?

- you saw someone stealing from the locker of a child you did not know?

- you saw someone give flowers to a teacher?

- you heard someone make cruel and unfair statements about a friend?

- you saw someone violently push a smaller child down on the playground?

Responses to these questions provide you with a glimpse of what your children are thinking. Please do not be critical of how a child responds. Encourage the child to elaborate on any comment before going to the next situation.

After helping her across a busy street, a police officer had gently touched the child's cheek, a parting gesture of friendliness to send her on her way. In the young girl's eyes, the police officer didn't simply touch her cheek, pat her cheek, or squeeze her cheek. He *caressed* her cheek. Consider what the word "caress" meant to the child, and what it meant for her to receive it from a man in uniform. What a discovery it must have been, to realize that she had finally arrived in a community where strangers cared.

Of course, not all police officers, or strangers, care. Even so, we should be more willing to look at each other through this child's eyes, eyes that had seen immense suffering caused by hate and social dislocation. Children need families to be a source of love and support through their lives. They also need a community to teach them to care beyond the borders of the familiar.

What a wonderful experience it would be if children could grow up in a community where they believed "there are no strangers here, only friends who have not yet met." Sadly, we live at a time when a cloud of suspicion hangs over the heads of all strangers, which means everyone. Fear can divide us and make us lose sight of the reality that we are all one people.

In *The Wizard of Oz*, the Tin Man sought a heart. He found it not in flesh and blood, but in tears of love. The Tin Man's sorrow was evidence of caring. Love is a risk, and caring can break our hearts. Even so, our lives become larger, not smaller, as we pull the circles of others toward our center. Only by stopping sometimes to expand our borders and draw another closer to ourselves can we achieve greatness. By stopping to listen to an elderly man's story of grief, or rushing to pull someone from a car stranded in front of an onrushing train, or returning to rescue a child from a dangerous intruder, young people have shown us that caring changes lives and brings warmth to a cold, indifferent world.

Step Three

From Danger to Vigilance

Key words:
fear, risk, safety, protection,
alertness, caution

Emphasis:
Be smart with your heart.

On the morning of April 24, 1997, eleven-year-old Christopher and his eight-year-old brother Tramell were waiting for the school bus at a stop near Milford, Kansas. Three Rottweiler dogs had escaped their enclosure at a nearby home, and began threatening the boys. Christopher and Tramell fled to the safety of the branches of a nearby tree, out of reach of the dogs' snapping jaws. The dogs then wandered away.

When he saw the bus approaching in the distance, Christopher told his younger brother that he would leave the tree to get help. Despite his brother's pleas to remain, Christopher climbed down and dashed toward the approaching bus.

The sudden movement alerted the Rottweilers. They reappeared and began chasing Christopher in front of the horrified bus driver and schoolchildren. The driver frantically attempted to position the bus to shield the young boy. Tragically, the Rottweilers pulled Christopher down and killed him before he could be rescued.[1]

Christopher reacted positively and decisively to danger. He felt the power, the push, to rescue his brother. He didn't run away to save himself—he died trying to get help. Christopher and his brother were smart to climb the tree. The mistake Christopher made was misunderstanding the greater danger of leaving his safe haven.

Danger and vigilance:
Be aware, beware, and be smart

Vigilance means "alertness to danger." Our vigilance provides a safe margin to evaluate alternative responses and make the best decision for action. When we nurture courage in children we must also ensure that vigilance is an element of their courage.

The speed of danger

The ability to think about danger and evaluate risk is affected by the timing of the threat. Danger can occur *suddenly*, without advance warning:

- a bully stops a child on the way to school and demands money;
- a toddler reaches for a pot of boiling water;
- a car swerves toward a classmate who is crossing a street.

Sudden danger requires swift decision making. The threat is immediate, and the risk of sudden danger is *panic*. Such danger is a test of speed and skill, similar to that of the sprinter.

Other forms of danger are more *persistent* and relentless:

- a student is frequently humiliated by her teacher in front of classmates;
- a family lives in darkness throughout the day because of their daughter's rare eye condition and painful sensitivity to light;
- a nine-year-old diabetic must monitor what he eats and remain alert to early signs of insulin shock.

Persistent danger requires endurance. Because the risk is predictable, there is time to think. The risk of persistent danger is *exhaustion* and *discouragement*. This is a test of endurance and spirit, like that of a long-distance runner.

The *Mighty Heart* portraits in this book reveal courage in response to sudden danger. As a former play therapist in a children's hospital, I saw many examples of courage by children (and their parents) who faced persistent danger, especially those with cystic fibrosis. Cystic fibrosis (CF) is an incurable disease caused by an inherited genetic defect. Children with cystic fibrosis suffer from chronic lung problems and digestive disorders. Their lungs become covered with sticky mucus that is difficult to remove and promotes bacterial infection. These children gradually drown in their own lung fluids, which are like silt filling up a water reservoir. Imagine trying to breathe with your lungs filled with rubber cement.

The life expectancy of people with CF used to be very short. Thirty years ago, most children with CF did not live beyond adolescence. Now, about 40 percent of all those affected by cystic fibrosis are eighteen years old or older. The median age of survival for a person with CF is 33.4 years. When I worked with CF children, parents had to provide vigorous and frequent physical therapy to loosen the mucus in their lungs. Every breath is a struggle. With this affliction, children have to be warriors to remain alive.

To see one's child suffer in a dreadful and relentless march toward death is a challenge that could cause despair in even the most devoted parent. Instead, I found a loving determination in these families. Amid the fight of their lives, these parents and children shared much happiness.

The importance of vigilance

The Carnegie Hero Fund Commission recognizes outstanding acts of selfless heroism performed in the United States and Canada. Andrew Carnegie established the fund in 1904, inspired by the heroism of two miners who acted courageously during a mine disaster that claimed 181 lives. In response to the tragedy and the sacrifices of these two men, Carnegie established a means for honoring and helping future "heroes of civilization."

In the years since, more than 8,764 rescuers have received a monetary grant and the Carnegie Hero Medal, which cites the commemorated deed and is inscribed with the biblical quotation "Greater love hath no man than this, that a man lay down his life for his friends" (John 15:13). Approximately 6 percent of Carnegie Hero Medal recipients have been younger than eighteen years. And about twenty percent of all awards were given posthumously.[2]

The Carnegie Hero Commission does not provide resources for teachers to publicize the names and stories of medal recipients to schoolchildren, nor does it consider education to be part of its mission. The Commission is concerned that promoting acts of heroism in public schools might encourage children to put themselves at risk, a concern that parents reading this book might share.[3]

All parents want to keep their children safe. The first duty of authority is to protect.[4] If we focus only on protection, however, we might actually be making our children *more* vulnerable to risk. Danger exists in the breathless moment of every heartbeat, at the top of a slide, in the menacing threats of a peer pushing drugs. We cannot plant our shield between our children and every danger.

We can protect our children *and* teach them to be vigilant by emphasizing being *smart with their hearts*. Being smart with the heart means combining caring with vigilance. Being alert to danger enables children to navigate risk without derailing the "prime mover" of the heart's call to action.

Nurturing vigilance

- **Provide a secure base of protection**
- **Teach children to be alert to danger**
- **Teach children to respect fear**
- **Teach children to evaluate danger**
- **Teach children to assess risk**
- **Teach children the fundamentals of first aid**
- **Teach children safety skills**

Scuffy the Tugboat, a children's classic written by Gertrude Crampton (Western, 1955), provided me with a favorite tale of boldness and caution during my childhood. "A toy store is no place for a red-painted tugboat. . . . I was meant for bigger things," Scuffy declares. So the man with the polka-dot tie and his son set the small boat on a gentle brook that quickly carries Scuffy downstream, away from his family.

At first, Scuffy is all too happy to embark on his solitary adventure. But he quickly discovers that the stream—and then the river, and finally the sea—can be dangerous places for a tiny tugboat. On his perilous journey Scuffy meets a curious cow, survives a dangerous logjam, and navigates a crowded port. To Scuffy's great relief, the man with the polka-dot tie rescues the little boat before he is pulled out into the ocean. Scuffy is happy to return to his safe and comfortable home.

Scuffy the Tugboat remains an example of two powerful and contradictory forces in our children. On one hand, they want to break free of parental restraint. Yet they also need a secure base of protection. The world entices children with its novelty and wonder. But danger lurks there as well.

Provide a secure base of protection

A troubled teenager gave a juvenile justice professional this reason for why he joined a gang: When he was a child, he witnessed a playground fight in which a stronger child tormented and then beat a smaller child. As the violent event unfolded, he saw a teacher watch the fight and then turn away. At that moment the boy concluded that he was essentially alone and unprotected if his teacher was afraid to intervene. He decided that the only way to be safe was to be a part of a gang.

The experience of being protected by a loving adult helps children understand that protecting others is important. Children need time to gain self-confidence and resilience. Children who experience the world as consistently dangerous will focus primarily on self-preservation and become uninterested in helping others.

We have to be careful not to undermine our children's self-confidence with overprotection. One of the kids in my neighborhood was never allowed to leave his front yard to play with the other boys. During grade school we regarded Ken as a tragic figure, friendless and lonely, unnaturally tethered to his home by an invisible rope. When he turned eighteen he left home to join the Navy.

Even as they increase their comfort zone of independence, children still need the security of vigilant parents. Watch a toddler and his mother in a coffee shop. While the mother talks to a friend, her confident child stretches the space between them while exploring the room.

The toddler is aware of his mother's presence. Both mother and child remain connected. As she talks with her friend, the mother follows her son's movement with vigilant eyes. As he gleefully stumbles from one chair to another, he occasionally stops to watch other customers intently. Then he makes eye contact with his mother at the table across the room and is reassured by her presence. He is free to stretch the boundaries between them because his mother occupies the watchtower.

Teach children to be alert to danger

The word "danger" originated from the Anglo-French term that meant not only harm but mastery. Danger challenges us to master a risk instead of being mastered by fear. If we hope to nurture vigilance in our children we have to do more than just talk about danger; we have to contribute to our children's

Mighty Heart
Wade Handsaker

On October 20, 1999, eighteen-year-old Wade Stirling Handsaker showed remarkable vigilance when he saved a seventy-year-old man from being killed by a train in Bellingham, Washington. The elderly man was in a motorized wheelchair that had become stuck at a crossing very close to the track of an approaching train. Moments earlier, Wade had bicycled past the man before he became stranded. Aware of the approaching train, Wade turned to check on the man's progress and saw his predicament. Wade immediately returned to the crossing, went to the man, and worked desperately to move him away from the track as the train bore down at undiminished speed. A projection of the lead locomotive struck the elderly man's lower left leg, severing it. He was taken to the hospital for treatment, where he recovered after rehabilitation. Wade was not hurt.[5]

mastery and their knowledge of how to respond to risk.

Vigilance begins with alertness to the existence of a threat. All of those described in the *Mighty Heart* portraits showed remarkable alertness to their surroundings. Fallon Richards recognized the danger when she noticed the smoke in her grandfather's mobile home. Keith Putnam and his friend saw the car stalled on the railroad tracks that night when others may have driven by without noticing.

Alertness is also important in the response to persistent danger. For example, asthmatic children have to be aware of conditions that could trigger an attack. Parents must be alert to the presence of teenage gangs in their neighborhoods.

Consider the vigilance of eighteen-year-old Wade Handsaker (see page 77). After passing an elderly man in a wheelchair, Wade stopped his bike and looked back to see if the man had crossed the railroad tracks safely. How many people would have continued on their way, not because of any ill will toward the elderly man but because they never bothered to stop and turn around? Wade saw that a train was approaching and that the man's wheelchair had become stuck in the tracks.

To encourage awareness, we might begin by discussing with our children what danger means. Consider these examples:

- An infant is poking at an electrical wall outlet. Her mother says, "No, no, Maria. That's *dangerous*. Do NOT put anything there!" (Points to socket.)

- A toddler reaches for a pot of boiling water. His dad shouts, "No, Jamal! *Dangerous.* Hot! Hot! That will hurt you!"

- A three-year-old runs into the street in front of his house. His mother tells him, "Bill, play in the yard! The street is *dangerous.*"

We can invite children as they grow older to be aware of potential threats in their surroundings. For example, we can take our five-year-old on an exploration of our home. We could ask, "If you were a crawling baby or a preschooler, is there anything that might be *dangerous* here?" We can engage them in these discussions in a playful yet serious way, careful not to exaggerate dangers that might or might not exist.

During the elementary school years, we can talk with children about dangers outside the home, such as:

- strangers who might ask them to get into a car;

- busy highways near home and school;

- bullies who might harass them;

- persuasive or charismatic peers who might encourage them to drink, do drugs, or engage in other risky behavior.

Teach children to respect fear

My school storytelling concerts, "A Time for Heroes," are usually held in an elementary school gym. Groups vary in size from rural schools of thirty children to urban groups of more than 600 students. Before telling my stories, I talk with children about courage and heroism. When I ask them what "courage" means, they often reply, "Courage means *not* being afraid." They reason that fear and courage are mutually exclusive. If you feel one, you cannot feel the other. My stories are intended to help them learn that courage is about *mastering* fear.

Spooky world
(preschool)

Take a few moments to talk with your children about what it means to be "frightened." Link the emotional experience with the presence of a threat. After discussing fear for a few moments, teach your young child the following action poem:

"When I'm feeling terrified,
(Make scared expression.)

the world seems so spooky.
(Look around.)

I want to find a place to hide—
(Put hands over head.)

maybe you could help me."
(Point to the child.)

Discuss with your child ways to help those who find themselves afraid. With older children, suggest they draw a picture or write a story about a time when they were frightened.

I tell them a story of a firefighter who enters a burning building to rescue a baby. I take their imaginations into the smoky house as flames curl along the ceiling and walls. The firefighter relentlessly searches every room, knowing that the house could collapse at any moment. Breathing is difficult and approaching flames hinder movement. After finding the baby, the firefighter struggles through the blinding smoke and blistering heat to reach safety just before the building collapses.

Immediately following the story I ask the children, "Did the firefighter feel afraid while looking for the baby?" They hesitate for a moment. Several children are about to say no, but catch themselves. A chorus of young voices then rises in agreement. Yes, the firefighter was afraid. *Yes, you can be brave and be afraid at the same time.*

Thinking about fear
(late preschool-elementary)

Ask children to define fear. What does it mean to "be afraid"? Introduce the idea that our minds tell us to be afraid. Sometimes what our minds tell us is true, other times it is not.

Ask children to give examples of people who are afraid. In each example, ask your children, "Is this fear based on good or bad judgment? How useful is fear in these circumstances?" (Create your own examples too.)

- You are afraid when you see an ant crawling on the sidewalk.

- You feel afraid near the edge of a cliff.

- You are afraid when the weatherman announces a tornado is approaching your town.

- You are afraid when a bully threatens you.

- You are afraid when a new classmate is seated next to you in school.

- You feel afraid when you see a strange dog.

Everyone can decide for themselves about whether their fear is correct or wrong. If a fear is correct, talk about why it is important. Fear can provide energy to the body. Fear can help us avoid danger. Ask your children whether fear in these examples is useful.

As we will see at Step Four (From Fear to Composure), fear is like a powerful stallion that can run away with us unless we control it. Once controlled, our fear shows us the dangers and pitfalls between us and our objective, making it possible for us to anticipate and avoid or conquer them. It mobilizes our physical strength and contributes to endurance. As Edmund Burke wrote, "Early and provident fear is the mother of safety." Fear speeds up our heartbeat and blood pressure, increases the supply of necessary sugar, and activates adrenalin and noradrenalin. Fear makes us more alert, and physically stronger and faster. The fear response is an evolutionary gift which contributes to self-preservation.

Teach children to evaluate danger

Once alert to a danger, children can then intelligently appraise their situation. Is it really dangerous? Children can make one of two mistakes in evaluating risk: first, incorrectly concluding that danger *does not* exist, and second, incorrectly concluding that danger *does* exist. Christopher made the first mistake when he climbed down from the tree. He made a tragic error when he thought he would be safe. A childhood story like *The Three Little Pigs* points out the risks of failing to recognize danger. Two of the three pigs believed their homes of straw and wood would withstand the wolf's attack. Only the smartest brother, in the brick home, would be safe. The second mistake, believing that there *is* danger where there is none, is illustrated by the tale of the main character ("Henny Penny") in *Chicken Little*, who thought the sky was falling after being hit by a stray object.

While these two mistakes define basic errors in perceiving danger, there is a third danger that we will call "self-deception." When someone senses that there is a problem but decides to ignore their intuition, they deceive themselves into a false sense of safety. *Little Red Riding Hood* is a classic cautionary tale about the danger of self-deception. Little Red Riding Hood knows there is something wrong ("Grandma, what big eyes you have!"). But each time she notices something unusual, she lets herself be fooled by the wolf's lies

("All the better to see you with, my dear!"). Little Red
Riding Hood is alert but fails to heed her intuition.

All children are at risk of making bad assessments
about potential danger due to their inexperience.
During my preschool years, my grandfather had a
Model T truck parked on a hill next to his home. That
old truck was a great place for a young child to play.
I spent hours pretending to drive. Oh, the places I
visited in that truck! However, as a four-year-old I was
blissfully unaware of the danger in pushing and
pulling various knobs and levers. Inevitably, one day I
accidentally released the parking brake. The truck
began to roll down the hill, picking up speed as I
desperately clung to the steering wheel. It careened
across a busy highway and then hurtled into a water-
filled ditch. Fortunately, I was unhurt. I crawled out the
window and over the hood to safety.

I ran back to the house to find my grandmother,
who was caring for me at the time. When I reported the
accident to her, at first she thought I was making up a
tall tale (something my grandfather loved to do). When
I insisted, she looked out her living room window to
see the front end of their truck sticking out of the ditch
at a 45-degree angle.

The inexperience that may lead children to be
oblivious to practical dangers is also conducive to an
awareness of impractical or unlikely danger. A child
may run screaming from a harmless bug. Another child
may be terrified by a circus clown. A third child
worries that all his blood is leaking from a cut.
Although their fears may seem humorous to adults,
children are serious about perceived danger.

Between three and five years of age, children's rich fantasy life contributes to a fear of darkness and the supernatural. Real dangers can be exaggerated by the imagination. When I was a graduate student in the Child Development Laboratory at Purdue University, I met a four-year-old who was terrified of wolves. Though wolves do not live in Indiana forests, he believed they lingered nearby, out of sight, ready to pounce and drag him into the woods. Because his fear was embedded deep in the limbic system of his brain, he was not reassured by our appeals to logic.

Then we discovered that the source of this fear was listening to the audiotape of the *Peter and the Wolf* story alone at home. Because he didn't hear the story told by a caring adult, he experienced his fear alone and without reassurance. As a result, his unrealistic fear grew out of control. Our task was to help him sort out fact from fiction about wolves. As he gained more information, he became more capable of discriminating between real and false danger.[6]

No stranger to danger
(late preschool-elementary)

Older children should be challenged to think about quick decisions in dangerous circumstances. This activity simulates the challenge of facing real dangers. Start with a challenge. Then ask your child to react (e.g., "You are walking by a house and see smoke coming out of the attic. What do you do?"). Next, ask the child to

Mighty Heart
Terreatha LeAnn Barnes

On April 19, 1992, eleven-year-old Terreatha LeAnn Barnes demonstrated risk management under pressure when she rescued a six-year-old and two other children from a runaway automobile in La Fayette, Georgia. The three children were inside a station wagon parked in a driveway when it began to drift backward toward the street. Terreatha saw the danger and immediately ran to the car. Catching up to it as it entered the street, she opened the front passenger door. As the car continued across the street, broke through a fence, and went over an embankment, she jumped head-first onto the front seat and applied the brakes with her hands, bringing the car to a stop. Requiring surgery for a fractured jaw sustained during the rescue, Terreatha was hospitalized overnight. She recovered.[7]

react to the potential consequences of the chosen action. Be as fair and as realistic as possible. Keep the tempo as fast as a child can manage to create a sense of urgency. When a solution has been achieved, go to a different situation. For example:

- You see an injured dog in a busy street.
- You see broken glass in the living room.
- You see an unattended stove turned on.
- You see a bully pushing another child who is unable to defend himself.
- You see a fire coming out of a house.

Choose situations appropriate to the child's age. In these dialogues, a child should experience a challenge but feel successful in his or her ability to think through the dangerous circumstances. When the conversation concludes, your child should feel more self-confident.

We should, however, be careful not to overlook children's capacity for imagination when teaching them about the way things really are. We teach children to be vigilant by inviting them to seek information to affirm or disprove the truth of their beliefs. Imagination enables children to think critically as well as inventively. Critical thinking can help children discover truth and move from irrational belief to rational knowledge about things that frighten them.

Teach children to assess risk

The decision to respond to danger should be influenced by one's assessment of the degree of risk involved in responding. If the danger is real, what is the best response? As they consider their capabilities, children may correctly estimate, overestimate, or underestimate both the extent of the danger and their capacity to succeed. Overestimating their power and underestimating the threat can result in unnecessary and reckless behavior. Many trips to the emergency room are the result of poor risk management by children. My five-year-old son split his eyebrow open when he tried jumping to the driveway from a stone wall. Bleeding profusely, he was rushed to the ER where he received ten stitches to close the gash. On the way home, his mother commented on how much it must have hurt. "Yeah," Bill replied, "for a while I thought I was a goner."

The opposite problem (underestimating their abilities and overestimating the threat) increases fear and results in a needless retreat from what a child can safely achieve. For example, a child might be too afraid to climb a slide or wade in the shallow end of a pool.

Eleven-year-old Terreatha Barnes (see page 86) demonstrated alertness, self-evaluation, and rapid risk assessment in her heart-stopping rescue of children in a runaway car. She made a correct estimate of what she could do to achieve success and recognized the danger to herself and the children in the car. She was smart with her heart.

Like others who have responded to sudden danger, she might be puzzled by questions about what she was thinking during the rescue. She might even claim that she didn't think at all. Even so, Terreatha made many decisions in the span of a few seconds, in a rapid-fire sequence that occurred just below the level of awareness. She had to judge the speed of the rolling vehicle, how fast she could get to it, and how to open the door and then apply the brake while the car remained in motion. Her brain must have lit up with concentration as she rushed forward. Yet if asked how she knew what to do, she might respond—as many such rescuers would—with a perplexed shrug.

Teach children the fundamentals of first aid

We can also teach children simple forms of first aid appropriate for their age. We might encourage a toddler to gently wash a sibling's tear-stained face. Four-year-olds can learn how to clean and apply a bandage on a simple scrape or cut. Some forms of first aid can be practiced on dolls or with parents who pretend to be sick. Grade school children should be encouraged to enroll in Red Cross first aid programs.

The ouchie
(preschool)

Gather a wet washcloth, a dry towel, a couple of small adhesive bandages, and something to use for fake blood. (Red tempera paint is good. Ketchup will also work.)

Bring your child into the bathroom or kitchen. Describe what happens when someone gets their skin cut. Ask: What is blood? Has he or she ever seen someone bleed? Talk about why bleeding is important. (The blood washes the wound and dries to form a natural bandage.) Sometimes we need to put a bandage on to help stop the bleeding.

Tell your child you are going to pretend that you are hurt. If the child is too young to understand the idea of pretend, then wait to do this activity until he or she is older. Take a small dab of the pretend blood and dab it on your finger. Say, "Oh look, I have a pretend cut on my finger. Can you help me?"

Talk your child through each of the steps, from cleaning and drying the "wound" to applying the bandage. Let your child do most of the work with only enough help to achieve success.

If you have more than one child, direct them to clean and bandage each other's "wounds."

Even young grade school children can apply life-saving first aid. On October 6, 1999, eight-year-old Austin Payne saved the life of his principal at Northridge Elementary School in Oklahoma City. Austin was in third grade. The principal was talking with a group of third graders during lunch in the cafeteria. The group had just told him not to talk with his mouth full, when they realized he could not speak.

He was choking on a piece of potato caught in his throat.

Austin bolted from his lunchroom chair and "squished up" behind the 175-pound man. He wrapped his hands around his waist and squeezed his stomach with two hard thrusts. Out popped the food that caused the choking. A few moments later, the principal was back at work. Austin learned the Heimlich technique from his father, Charlie Payne. What was Austin's response to the attention? "I just did what I had to do," he said.[8]

The American Red Cross Web site (www.redcross.org) provides many examples of young people who saved the lives of others through their training in first aid. For example, after running to catch a bus in Dover, Pennsylvania, a twelve-year-old suddenly collapsed after boarding. Fourteen-year-old Dominick Watts checked the boy's vital signs and found that he had a faint heartbeat and shallow breathing. While the bus driver called for help, Dominick checked the boy's vital signs again and discovered that his heart had stopped beating and he no longer had a pulse. Dominick and another student carried the boy off the bus and began CPR. A police officer arrived shortly thereafter and assisted Dominick with his lifesaving efforts until an ambulance arrived.

The police officer reported that Dominick ". . . was just very knowledgeable in the process. I didn't have to coach him. He was doing compressions and the counting; it was textbook-like. He performed like a veteran." After visiting the boy whose life he saved, Dominick said, "I had to see that what I did made a difference; I feel a lot better knowing the younger boy survived."[9]

Teach children safety skills

Children should be taught safety skills appropriate to their age. Instead of telling them what *not to do,* emphasizing safety skills helps children learn what *to do* to be safe. Safety fundamentals might include

- where to play outside the home;
- how to cross a street at a red light;
- how to safely ride a bike;
- how to buckle up when riding in a car;
- how to put on a life vest when in a boat.

Parents can also encourage children to think about alternatives for responding to danger. For example, they could think of different ways to respond

- to a storm or fire;
- if someone is unconscious or hurt;
- if a stranger wants them to get into his car;
- if classmates try to hurt them.

The Red Cross offers courses for children that include junior lifeguarding, child care, emergency first aid, and many other useful life skills. They often provide certificates of accomplishment for children to display. Learning safety skills can do more than save a child's life. They also prepare children to take effective action when someone else might also be in danger. A child who knows what to do in an emergency can also be a significant help in calming fearful younger children.

By teaching alertness, mastery of fear, and safety skills, we provide children with the shield, stallion, and armor that they will need to achieve vigilance. *Alertness* is the shield that allows them to take time to observe and gain information about the threat. *Mastery of fear* is the stallion that does not panic on the field, but harnesses fear to survive. *Safety skills* are the armor that protect our children while giving them the ability and wisdom to succeed.

Step Four

From Fear
to Composure

Keywords:
calm, endurance, self-control,
panic, emotional hijacking,
depression, restraint

Emphasis:
Stay in control in an
emotional storm.

It was a hot summer night in 1952. A terrified six-year-old sat upright in his bed, desperately gasping for air. He could barely breathe. His chest was a vise, squeezing the life out of him. Asthma medication that would clear his lungs and enable him to breathe had not yet been invented. He rocked himself back and forth, wondering if he was going to die. He fought panic, the great enemy, by praying with his rosary beads clutched in his hand. He wanted to avoid waking his mother. The rhythm of the prayer helped him relax and the asthma gradually subsided. Only then did he risk lying back on his pillow to seek a restless sleep.

That night, I won the battle between panic and composure.

Fear is a natural response to danger and an ingredient in courage. Consider the case of Aaron Hall (page 97). When Aaron first saw the cougar, his senses became hypersensitive, and he froze for a moment. Aaron's skeletal muscles tensed and began metabolizing glycogen to provide extra fuel. His cardiovascular system sped up the pumping of blood as his body temperature and blood pressure elevated. His digestion slowed. Aaron's breathing changed as he inhaled air more deeply and more frequently to carry more oxygen to his muscles.

As he began moving toward the cougar, Aaron became drenched with sweat as his body attempted to prevent overheating. His pupils dilated to let in more light and enhance peripheral vision. He may have had a sudden urge to empty his bladder and bowels as his body refocused its resources to respond to the danger. His body hairs stood on edge, similar to a cat puffing itself up when threatened. All this happened in what seemed like a tenth of the time it takes to blink, without any conscious thought.[1]

If Aaron had been cut in the struggle, his blood would have clotted more quickly to stem the bleeding.

Mighty Heart
Aaron Hall

While attending day camp in Missoula, Montana, on July 31, 1998, a group of hikers entered an isolated forest. A ninety-two-pound mountain lion suddenly appeared and attacked a six-year-old boy, taking him to the ground and biting him on the neck. Aaron M. Hall, a sixteen-year-old counselor, responded immediately. He rushed the animal and began screaming and kicking dirt at the mountain lion's face.

As the lion began to drag the six-year-old by the neck into the woods, Aaron continued his own ferocious attack to save the boy's life. The mountain lion then released his grip on his young victim and backed off to snarl at Aaron. Aaron charged the animal once again, screaming and kicking until it fled into the forest. The six-year-old survived the attack despite severe wounds to his face and neck. Aaron was unhurt.[2]

Natural opiate-like compounds would have been released into his blood stream to blunt his pain. But now a longer pathway of awareness reached the thinking part of his brain. He became totally focused on the behavior of the cougar, the desperation and position of the little boy, and potential avenues of escape for both animal and human. He made a rapid sequence of decisions. He looked for anything he could use for a weapon. Finding none, he began kicking and screaming at the animal. Though his actions may have been reflexive, they were the product of the neurological processes underlying fear.

Emotional hijacking and composure

The six-year-old hiker benefited from the physical power of Aaron's emotional response. More importantly, he was rescued because Aaron was able to channel this power by making smart decisions. Fear is a healthy response to danger. Fear originates in the center of the brain, from a group of neural structures called the limbic system. Unabated, fear can increase until it causes an emotional blindness that can result in panic.

In addition to the limbic system, there is a slower "track" of thinking in the brain behind and above the eyes called the prefrontal cortex. The slower path of thinking can engage and moderate the fast loop of emotion by providing information and evaluation. If the emotional loop does not benefit from rational thinking, then emotion can spin out of control in what neurophysiologists call *emotional hijacking*.

A mother described her earliest memory of managing fear. As a young city girl, she enjoyed visiting her grandparents' farm. One morning when she was five years old, her grandmother took her into the chicken coop to gather eggs. A startled hen jumped from its perch onto her head and began to squawk and flap its wings. Even though the grandmother swiftly removed the hen from the child's hair, the young girl was terrified by the experience.

When she returned to visit the following summer, her grandmother asked her to gather eggs. Despite her fear, the six-year-old agreed to the responsibility. Early the next morning, she stood outside the chicken coop door alone, trembling and afraid. She took a deep breath, shook off her dread, and opened the door. The smell of hay, the sound of clucking, and the restless movement of chickens were ominous greetings that set her heart pounding. The air seemed to be sucked out of the room. Fighting panic, she moved as quickly and carefully as she could to gather the eggs. Then she dashed from the coop and shut the door firmly behind her. Immense relief washed over her. She had survived!

She also felt proud of herself for completing her duty. She chose to act despite the fear. Even though her act of courage would never make local headlines, she felt great self-respect when she closed that door behind her. Aristotle wrote, "Dignity consists not in possessing honors but in the awareness that we deserve them."

Emotional hijacking in response to sudden danger can result in three different reactions. Some people flee. Some never get past a state of maladaptive freezing, unable to recover from a paralyzing shock. Some act blindly and put themselves or others in greater danger.

Emotional hijacking in response to *persistent* danger has much different consequences. In these cases, a person can give up and become depressed, or act in irrational and destructive ways. Facing danger, loss, and unalleviated fears over an extended period of time can produce a kind of "combat fatigue," in which well-being is gradually eroded by acute anxiety and depression, profound weariness, abandonment of positive beliefs, and a general loss of will to survive.

Children gradually acquire *composure* through a process of emotional self-regulation.[3] Learning composure is a gradual process that begins in the first days of life. Consider Maria, a healthy child in a loving family. By three months Maria stops crying when her mother enters the room. At six months she looks sad and puckers her lips before crying. When she is upset she rubs her special blanket and her hair to calm herself. At nine months she turns away from her father's scowl to soothe herself. At one year, when she bumps her knee and begins crying, she calms down when her father gently holds her. At eighteen months, Maria can stop herself for at least twenty seconds when her mother tells her to not take the wrapping paper off her gift. By two years she pauses in conversations with her parents to let them have a turn speaking. As a three-year-old, she recovers from her temper tantrums within ten minutes and she has fewer of them.[4] Before she begins to get upset, Maria will now distract herself from crying by choosing to play with one of her toys.

At four, even though she feels sad, Maria separates from her parents for short periods without crying. When she is with other children, she takes turns when playing and shares her toys, though not always without protest. At six she knows it's not acceptable to laugh out loud in church. At eight she stops herself from crying on the school playground to avoid being ridiculed. She smiles and acts like she enjoys the food a friend's mother prepared even though she dislikes the taste. By early adolescence, Maria can calm her fear before going on stage in a school play.

The ability to delay gratification is one facet of self-regulation. The ability of preschoolers to control their impulses has long-term implications. Walter Mischel and his colleagues at Stanford University devised an experiment in which four-year-olds were tested for their ability to delay gratification.[5] The children were told they could have two marshmallows if they waited until the experimenter returned from an errand. One marshmallow was placed on a dish in front of the child. The experimenter told the child that if he or she couldn't wait, it was all right to eat it before the experimenter returned, but then the child couldn't get the second marshmallow.

Two-thirds of the children waited. To distract themselves from the temptation of eating the marshmallow, some sang to themselves, others made up games to play at the table. Some even covered their eyes. One-third of the children grabbed and ate the marshmallow as soon as experimenter left the room.

Fourteen years later, the researchers revisited their original subjects. They discovered that adolescents who were impulse-resistant as four-year-olds were better able to cope with frustration, less impulsive, and more confident, assertive, and successful in human relationships. The impulsive grabbers tended to be more stubborn, indecisive, mistrustful, envious, argumentative, and pugnacious. As children become more capable in self-regulation they become more capable of facing significant risks and sacrifices with courage.

All of those with *Mighty Hearts* whose stories are retold in this book were able to act decisively because they were able to control and channel their emotions. Instead of becoming preoccupied with their personal anxiety, they transcended fear when someone needed them.

Nurturing composure

- **Provide an example of emotional mastery**
- **Use a calming touch, voice, and motion when children are upset**
- **Maintain reassuring routines**
- **Increase positive self-talk and reduce inflammatory self-talk**
- **Give children something positive to do when they feel afraid**
- **Provide opportunities for children to practice emotional restraint**

A four-year-old stands at the bottom steps of the slide, gazing fearfully at the steps rising upward to the sky. Her heart trembles and her hands are sweaty. She hears the encouraging words of her father. "You can do it, Nevaeh!" When the moment arrives, it feels as though the direction of her life will be decided by her choice to move forward or retreat. This instant is a decisive pause. She sighs and reaches out to grasp the railing, tentatively at first and then more firmly. She looks up and her eyes brighten in concentration. She takes one step, then another, and then another, confidence slowly building. Her heart is pounding like a snare drum and her knees are as wobbly as Jell-O, but still she climbs up. She reaches the top, higher than she has ever gone before without the reassuring grasp of Mother or Father. Then another decisive moment and she rockets down the slide into the arms of her father. Her life will never be the same.

Nevaeh is learning composure, the self-regulation of fear. She is by nature a cautious and emotional child. Her parents have learned to work with her temperament to help her gradually gain control over her fears at her own pace.

Provide an example
of emotional mastery

One of the most important things we can do to contribute to composure in our children is to gain and demonstrate control over our own emotions. By the end of their first year, children use "social referencing" to modify their behavior.[6] They become increasingly aware of how their parents control their own emotions. Displays of intense emotional states are contagious. Children begin shaping their emotional response based on the behavior of their parents. For example, a four-year-old might be afraid of being near a friendly, gentle dog. After seeing the parent smile and approach the animal, the child might do likewise. The parent pets the dog and tells the child, "See, Amos is a nice dog. See his tail wag? He wants us to pet him. We can do that gently. See?" By watching and listening to her parent, the child moves closer and hesitantly touches the animal's head. She borrows a small portion of the parent's boldness to manage her initial anxiety.

Parents' emotions serve as cues. For example, a toddler runs across a yard and falls within sight of his mother. He looks at her face. Does she show alarm and concern? If so, the toddler's anxiety skyrockets and he begins crying. If she responds calmly, he may laugh if he was more frightened than hurt. He trusts her evaluation of his tumble.

Fear and anger in parents can have a chilling effect on children. A mother who is apprehensive about separation from her four-year-old is likely to contribute to her child's fear when he starts preschool. A father who panics at the sight of bugs is likely to raise children who have a similar fear unless they have a more positive role model. Parents who display high levels of anger at home raise angry and disobedient children.[7]

Emotional hijacking in parents provides an unstable role model for children. Several years ago, a young mother and two preschool children were caught in a blizzard one night as they drove along I-70 near my hometown of Manhattan, Kansas. The mother was under great stress to get to her destination. Because they were tired and anxious, both children were complaining and fussing with each other. The mother's pleas for quiet were unsuccessful. Her demands became louder and more desperate. Then she arrived at her breaking point. She told both children that she would make them get out of the car if they continued arguing.

When the misbehavior continued, the mother's fear and anger overwhelmed her logic. In a moment of rage, her thinking brain shut down and she became emotionally blind. She stopped the car and made both children get out in the snowstorm. Then she drove away. Fortunately, a police officer was nearby and rescued both children. The officer then sped up and arrested the woman for child neglect. She insisted that she was only trying to scare the children and was going to turn around and pick them up at the first opportunity. Both children were placed in temporary foster care.

This sudden loss of control is terrifying to both children and onlookers. While helping to feed babies in the hospital nursery where I worked as a play therapist I saw a father grow increasingly frustrated with his toddler, who was refusing to eat. All of his frantic pleas to his baby to eat were met with resistance. Then he began to raise his voice and become more demanding. The child began to cry. At this point, I should have stopped to help this anxious father. To my regret, I didn't. As his voice and the child's wails became more strident, the father suddenly lashed out and slapped the child's face. Then he rose from his chair and fled from the room. His emotions overwhelmed his ability to think rationally.

These parents had reached a point where the emotional alarms were ringing so loudly that they had become unable to think. Emotional hijacking is not an excuse for their poor choices. Making a mistake, though, does not make someone a bad person. Each of us has a breaking point. Learning composure protects us from letting our emotions blind us from taking intelligent action.

Being composed does not mean achieving a state of tranquility free of anger, sadness, and fear. Composure means maintaining the ability to respond gracefully even when under pressure. As the poet Shelley wrote, "Man who man would be, must rule the empire of himself." Our children learn to rule themselves by observing this talent in those they love and respect.

Use a calming touch, voice, and motion when children are upset

Children gradually learn composure by borrowing the strength of their parents. Young children cannot manage panic, grief, or rage entirely on their own. When they are held, rocked, and sung to, most children experience a physiological change as their brains trigger hormones that calm the negative emotion. With every repetition of this soothing experience, children's brains become more capable of self-soothing. The rise and fall of cascading emotions is a workout for the brain.

During my worst asthma attacks, my mother often took me outside in the middle of the night to the front porch of our Detroit home. As I sat bundled up in her lap, she would talk and sing to me. The cool night air and her reassuring touch enabled me to relax so I could go back to sleep.

This experience enabled me to help myself when she was not there. My brain had learned what to do. Loving touches and calming voices have an effect on physiology. Distressed children who hear the soothing songs of parents may later sing to themselves to calm themselves down when their parents are absent.

By the end of kindergarten, children need less continuous adult support and guidance to maintain control. By age seven, they should be capable of reliable internal self-regulation of behavior and emotional expression. They make the shift from predominantly external to internal control.[8] The relationship between parental support and learning composure is similar to a parent helping a child learn to ride a bicycle before letting the child go off on his own.

In Denys Cazet's gentle book *Christmas Moon* (Bradbury Press, 1984), a young bunny is unable to sleep because of grief over the death of his grandfather. Instead of trying to stop the sadness, the mother aligns herself with her child's grief. She sits and talks with him about his loss and shares her sadness. Once she demonstrates that she understands, she introduces a new element into the discussion. She teaches her son *moon magic*, something her grandfather taught her when she was young that chases the sadness away.

. . . Mother turned off the light.

She waved her hand through the moonlight and wiggled her fingers over Patrick.

She ran her fingers through his hair and hugged him tightly. She kissed him on the cheek.

"Moon magic," said mother.

As she shared her memories of his grandfather, Patrick's mother accomplished two things. First, her calm, reassuring touches and hugs eased Patrick's distress. Second, she shared a memory of his grandfather that provided a soothing mental image that helped him settle into a peaceful sleep.

Observation of human infants with little nurturing contact reveals how their lives deteriorate. When no one responds to their needs for touch and motion, infants will first protest. They will cry. As neglect continues, stress hormones flood their brains, upsetting delicate neurophysiological checks and balances. Widespread disruption of bodily rhythm results: their heart rate slows and the level of growth hormone plummets, their circadian (twenty-four hour) rhythms are disrupted, and immunity drops.[9]

If the neglect is severe enough, their brains become unable to recover from stress, synaptic connections between neurons deteriorate, and ultimately nerve cells in their brains die, never to be replaced. Children who are rarely touched develop brains that are twenty to thirty percent smaller than normal for their age.[10] James Garbarino found that the experience of early trauma leads boys to become hypersensitive to arousal in the face of threat and to respond to such threats by disconnecting emotionally or acting out aggressively.[11]

Maintain reassuring routines

Life without satisfying routines that provide stable anchors in a busy day can be stressful and chaotic for children. Consider these examples of daily routines:

- Every morning mom wakes up her children with a hug and the words, "Rise and shine!"

- The entire family sits down for supper at about the same time every evening.

- Father reads a bedtime story to his children every night.

- Mother tucks her children into bed and gives them a kiss every night.

- Mother waves to her children when they leave for school.

Goodnight sweet child
(all ages)

Do your children have comforting routines when they go to bed at night? Reexamine what you and your children do together. Begin a new ritual if you can think of something more satisfying. You might say a traditional prayer together (but avoid the ". . . if I die before I wake" prayer). You could invite your children to make up a short prayer. You could sing a brief bedtime song, such as "Hush Little Baby." Be sure to include an action that brings you into contact with your children—a hug, a touch to the cheek, a tuck of the covers around the child's chin.

You can even start a special good-night journal for your child by keeping a spiral notebook in which the child can write someting special that happened that day before going to bed. (You can write the date and the child's words in the journal yourself until they can write it down themselves.) Whether it's something as minor as "We had chocolate pudding for desert" or as major as "Today was my birthday party," jotting down positive recollections before bed is a fun way to end the day on a graceful note. These notebooks will be treasures later on. Your adult child ·may keep them in a trunk and enjoy reading them when the warmth of those memories might chase away her blues.

No matter what you choose for a routine, keep it short and simple so you can do it every night. If there is more than one child in the bedroom, do the same thing for both.

Continue the ritual with grade-schoolers, modified for their continued enjoyment. Children do not outgrow the need for this parental reassurance before falling asleep.

This bedtime transition is a quiet moment that children find reassuring at any age. Relaxing at the end of the day with you may also provide them with an opportunity to talk with you about their worries.

Every family will have different kinds of reassuring routines. Of course, no routine can be counted on 100 percent of the time. Father or Mother may travel or the family may be on vacation. The best routines are stable experiences that establish a familiar rhythm in children's lives. A father who tells stories to his children at bedtime will be sorely missed when he leaves on military duty for several months. When he returns, though, his children will eagerly look forward to their special times with him again.

Increase positive self-talk and reduce inflammatory self-talk

We all engage in self-talk ("conversation with oneself") when we have a decision to make. Sometimes our self-talk is silent, words spoken to ourselves but not uttered. Sometimes self-talk is spoken aloud as though hearing the words invests them with more power. What children say to themselves in either way when they are frightened, sad, or angry can have a significant effect on their composure.

Private or "subvocal" speech is observable in children between the ages of three and five years. This self-talk becomes increasingly important in controlling behavior by delaying gratification and serving as a means for self-guidance and problem solving. For example, a mother asks her three-year-old son to keep his hands away from a freshly baked batch of cookies sitting on the kitchen table. She leaves the room for few moments. She peeks into the kitchen and sees him look longingly at the plate of delicious cookies. Then he puts his hands behind his back and says quietly to himself, "No cookies. Mama say no cookies."

Positive self-talk contributes to composure while negative self-talk increases arousal. We make predictions to ourselves of likely success or failure. Imagine taking a thick plank and laying it flat in your yard. You could probably walk across the length of that plank without falling off. Now imagine that the same plank securely spans the towers of a cathedral. Would you approach the walk differently? Consider the difference in your self-talk and how it would affect you emotionally. If we faced walking the plank with the ground far below, must of us would find our knees wobbling and our heart pounding. Even though the task is essentially the same, what we tell ourselves at that moment is likely to make a difference in how we perform.

Supportive words told to children during an emotional experience may someday be incorporated into their self-talk:

- "Maria! I know your heart is beating fast, but you can do it!"
- "Jason, you can do this safely!"
- "Martina, you're a smart girl. Figure it out!"

When I talk with children about finding courage when bullied, I tell a story in which a character's grandfather teaches her the following rhyming self-affirmation: "When you are afraid of the bully's might, just take a deep breath and do what's right!"

Give children something positive to do when they feel afraid

Effective action is often the best tonic for turbulent emotions. In some cases, the action refocuses our children's attention on something other than how they feel. A mother told me how she gave her three-year-old something positive to do when he complained about monsters in his room in the middle of the night. She put some water in an old perfume bottle and gave it to him to keep nearby. She told him the mist was "monster spray" that would make the monsters go away. Her child found the spray reassuring and empowering and did not complain about the monsters again. The child used an imaginary solution to deal with an imaginary problem.

Dream allies
(late preschool-elementary)

The next time your child wakes up from a nightmare, comfort her first. Then, instead of telling her it's *just* a dream, invite her to return to the dream when she falls back asleep to confront the scary thing. In simple, gentle words encourage the child to follow the principles attributed to the Senoi tribes of Malaysia:[12]

- Do not run from danger in a dream.

- Turn and face whatever is frightening you.

- If there is a frightening creature in your dream, confront it. Stare into its eyes; overfeed it to make it helpless; force it to perform some activity that exhausts it; make friends with it by petting it; most importantly, talk to it and ask what it wants and why it is unfriendly.

- If you need help in your dream, call on a familiar ally (a pet dog, a stuffed animal come to life, a parent or grandparent) to help you fight against the creature until more help arrives.

- Once the dream enemy has been confronted and conquered, it must give you a gift.

- Instead of suppressing the dream, the message in this tradition is, "You can face it; you are a strong person. This is what you must do."

A parent might help a fearful child select and wrap a gift for her teacher on the first day of school. The activity could provide her with a distraction from her fear and give her something to do before she has to leave for school. A grandmother provided her young grandson with a small angel pin when he had nightmares about ghosts after his older brother died. She reassured him that his brother was now an angel he could call on for help in his nightmares. She pinned the angel on his pajamas as a reassuring talisman, a reminder that his brother's spirit would protect him from supernatural dangers.

In some cases, our children may take more direct action. My daughter overcame her fear of being unable to defend herself from bullies by learning karate. *Mighty Heart* Ronald Fischer (see page 115) took heroic action in the middle of the night to try to save his mother from her attacker. The fifteen-year-old did not hide under his covers. He didn't run away. When he took control of his emotions he took action.

In *Harry and the Terrible Whatzit* (Houghton Mifflin, 1978), Dick Gackenbach writes about a young child, Harry, who is afraid of the monster who lives in his home. Harry is certain something terrible lives in the dark, smelly cellar. When his mother goes to the basement and fails to return, Harry summons his courage to rescue her. When he confronts the Terrible Whatzit in the basement Harry makes an interesting

Mighty Heart
Ronald Fischer

On July 21, 2000, fifteen-year-old Ronald Fischer was asleep in his bedroom on the second floor of his family's Michigan home. He awoke to his mother's screams. He rushed to the kitchen, and discovered a man repeatedly stabbing her. Ronald immediately jumped on the man's back to defend his mother. During the ensuing struggle, the attacker turned on Ronald, stabbing him in the chest. Despite his wound, Ronald continued to struggle to stop the assault. After sustaining another stab wound, Ronald realized that he could not overcome the attacker alone. So he ran from the house to seek help. Unfortunately, the trauma he had experienced overcame him, and he collapsed in a neighbor's yard. After fleeing the scene by car, the attacker was quickly apprehended by police. Ronald was taken to the hospital and eventually recovered from his wounds. Sadly, his mother died of her injuries despite his heroic defense.[13]

discovery: The creature shrinks if his intended victim is not frightened by its threats. The more Harry stands up to the monster, the more it shrinks until it is forced to flee.

Provide opportunities for children to practice emotional restraint

Children learn composure gradually. Exposure to too much fear can overwhelm the mind's capacity to evaluate information and make decisions. We can help children take small steps that build confidence to prepare them for overcoming larger fears. For example, consider a five-year-old who is terrified of water. Jeremy's dad knows that forcing him into the water at the lake will only make him more terrified. So he begins by inviting Jeremy to wade with him at the shallow end of the city pool. But Jeremy is still too frightened to enter the water. So his father asks him to sit with him at the edge of the pool with his legs in the water, something Jeremy is willing to do. During a future visit, Jeremy might be willing to wade in the shallow end as his confidence increases. Eventually, he may allow water up to his waist as long as his dad is nearby. As his progress continues, he may be willing to separate from his dad and eventually take swimming lessons.

Still water
(preschool)

 Ask your child to splash water. You could be washing dishes at the sink, helping draw the child's bath, or swimming at the local pool.

Splash and swirl the water together, adding exciting sound effects. Woosh! Kersplash! Swish! Then ask the child to stop and stay quiet. What happens to the water? The waves settle down into the surface. Say something like, "Now it's *still water.*" Repeat this action and statement several times. Make sure the child understands what the words "still water" mean.

Then when your child is upset, take him or her by the hand and gently say, "Still water." If the child is confused, remind him of the game, and end by making a smoothing gesture with your arms, saying "Still water." The words "still water" can become associated with composure. If you do this often enough at the correct times, your children may say the phrase by themselves to regain their poise in a moment of stress.

This process takes patience. When Jeremy was a toddler, he slipped in the bathtub and his face went under the water when he bumped his head. His mother's panicked response heightened his fear. Since that event, Jeremy could not rationally think his way out of being afraid of water. The original fear was too strong and outside the reach of his rational mind. With the help of his father, Jeremy was able to chip away gradually at the stone wall of his fear.

Even in cases where we think the fear is irrational, we need to respect our children's internal voice. But acceptance and respect do not mean approval. If we think children are afraid due to a misconception, we can encourage them to gather information to put their fears into perspective.

Courage depends on bringing a rich emotional response to life. Composure is a gathering of power in the moment before decisive action. The firefighters who went up the steps at the World Trade Center, Aaron Hall, Ronald Fischer, and all the *Mighty Hearts* described in this book felt the icy grasp of fear. Like Max in *Where the Wild Things Are*, they looked in the eyes of the beast with a resolute heart and said, "BE STILL!" Only then, when they mastered the turbulence within, could they take a deep breath and ride the whirlwind to greatness.

Step Five

From Self
to Empathy

Keywords:
compassion, insight, sympathy,
suffering

Emphasis:
Let yourself be touched by the
suffering of others.

I once met a remarkable three-year-old during an airline flight. She and her young mother sat by the window next to my seat. After reading her daughter a story, the mother fell asleep. The child continued to entertain herself, singing quietly and playing with her hands. Then something remarkable happened that I still find difficult to explain.

A child about seven rows in front of us began to cry. The cries quickly intensified to terrified screeching. While this was happening the little girl next to me stopped what she was doing, suspended breathlessly in mid-action. She appeared to be concentrated on listening. I found the screams quite alarming, but just before I called the flight attendant the young girl next to me said cheerfully, "Oh, he's just pretending!" At that moment, almost as if on cue, the other child's screams dissolved into laughter.

I was stunned. How could this three-year-old have known that the other child was not distressed? What had I, a developmental child psychologist, overlooked? I was, and still am, in awe of the sensitivity this child displayed. When the mother woke up, I told her what had happened. I also told her that I thought her child's response was remarkably perceptive.

What is empathy?

This young girl displayed amazing empathy. Empathy is bringing one's own experience into harmony with that of another. We set aside a preoccupation with our personal thoughts and feelings to focus harmoniously on the life of another person. The child next to me on the airline flight resonated to emotional tones of the crying child that I had missed. She felt what the other child felt.

Imagine two tuning forks. Gently strike one and hold it close to the other. If they are in tune, the one not struck will begin to vibrate and make its sound. In the same way, the sadness of someone we care about brings tears to *our* eyes even though we are not the one struck with pain. We see her experience from her perspective. Empathy means being in tune with someone.

There are two complementary forms of empathy: compassion and insight. *Compassion* is activated in the *emotional* core of the brain known as the limbic system. The origin of the word "compassion" is in the Latin *cum pati*, which means "to suffer with." Compassion also means sharing another's distress or delight. A father claps and shouts with joy when his toddler proudly shows him the tower he built from blocks. A mother's face reflects the anxiety of her ten-year-old when he walks out on stage at his school play. Both are examples of compassion.

Compassion is not a conscious choice. It arrives unbidden, a spontaneous gift of caring. We cannot force ourselves, or our children, to feel compassion. Watch the faces of mothers and fathers when their children are sad, scared, or happy. Do their faces become animated with emotion that mirrors the emotions of their children? Will we see on their faces the pain their children feel when they are hurt, and the joy, they radiate when they are happy?

Are your children learning compassion? While reading or telling a story to them, watch their faces. As your face and voice convey anger, sadness, fear, and joy, do your children's faces reflect similar emotion?

As we can see in the developmental milestones, compassion can arrive early in a child's life. Babies will "tune in" to our emotions. They react in different ways to our happy and sad facial expressions. At nine months, they can even understand subtle emotional differences in our voices. In a loving, supportive environment where their emotions are respected, they quickly begin to resonate to how we feel.

In contrast to compassion, *insight* is primarily *intellectual*. We view another's experience from his or her perspective. Insight is aroused in the thinking part of the brain, the area called the *prefrontal cortex*. The capacity for insight begins at about two years old. Young children are more likely to show compassion before their brains have matured sufficiently to transform experience into insight. A two-year-old's eyes may brim with tears, for example, when seeing his mother cry without understanding why she feels so sad.

Compassion and insight motivate kindness. Feeling another person's suffering without being overwhelmed by it fuels the ability to react with wisdom and kindness. Insight about the circumstances enables us to tune our response to provide effective help. A mother of a four-year-old reported that her son gave his beloved teddy bear to a child he did not know who was heartbroken when his toy broke. The other child's tears had aroused her son's sadness. An understanding of the other child's plight provided her son with a solution. He could ease the other child's distress by giving him his teddy bear.

Eva Fogelman, in her research on courage, discovered that children and adults who take risks to help others have often experienced a form of suffering that creates a bond between themselves and the person in danger. Irene Gut, a nineteen-year-old Polish nursing student during World War II, revealed both compassion and insight in response to the suffering she witnessed. One day the young woman and her sister heard shooting from the restaurant where she and her sister worked as waitresses. They were both excused from work because the experience was so distressing.

Mighty Heart
Dennis Carter

On the night of December 28, 2000, twelve-year-old Dennis Lorenzo Carter responded with compassion and courage to save a seventy-nine-year-old man from a burning building in Martinsville, Virginia. The elderly man was in the living room of his second-floor apartment when fire broke out on the first floor and filled the building with smoke. Unable to walk unaided, he broke out a living room window and called for help. Dennis saw smoke coming out of the building, then saw the desperate man leaning out the window. Dennis rushed through an outside door to the man's apartment. Despite dense smoke that extended almost to the floor, he crawled inside the room. Unable to find the man quickly, Dennis had to retreat for air. He crawled inside again and found him. By this time, another man had also entered the apartment to help. As flames spread quickly through the building, Dennis and his co-rescuer brought the elderly man outside to safety. The building was destroyed by the fire. The victim required hospitalization for treatment of smoke inhalation, and Dennis, too, was treated at the hospital for smoke inhalation. They both recovered.[1]

On their way home, she saw Jews being shot in front of shallow graves. "The earth was shaking with the breath of those who had been buried alive," she wrote later. At that moment, she made a covenant with God, asking for an opportunity to help even at the risk of her life. Irene eventually saved the lives of twelve Jews and smuggled food out to two hundred more hiding in a forest.[2]

Empathic responses were especially keen in rescuers who had grieved a death or significant personal loss in childhood. In her interviews of rescuers, Fogelman discovered that a majority of those who rescued Jews admitted to having undergone at least one traumatic experience in childhood.[3] Samuel and Pearl Oliner also found that rescuers of Jews during the Second World War were definitely more empathic and more easily moved by pain than nonrescuers, and 37 percent attributed their first helping act to an empathic reaction.[4]

Nurturing empathy

- **Resonate to children's emotions**
- **Use "emotion" words**
- **Focus children's attention on the emotions of others**
- **Allow children to experience spontaneous feelings of compassion**
- **Show children how to be empathic**

Empathy originates early in life and develops in tandem with the quality of the child's interpersonal relationships. Correspondingly, children who are incapable of empathy have previously experienced a disconnection in nurturing relationships followed by a detachment in caring. They cannot be aroused to action or compassion in the face of the suffering, having no internal template of their own on which to base such a response.

Jason was one of the few children I taught who seemed unable to experience compassion. During the year he was in my preschool class, I never saw this four-year-old cry or laugh. He was a loner who would push other children down and impassively watch his victims cry. Several parents were calling for his removal.

After another aggressive incident, I took Jason aside and confronted him eye-to-eye. While holding him gently by the shoulders, I said, "Jason, you know that pushing Mark was wrong. You hurt him when you did that. Did you see his tears? I will not let you hurt others here. I care about you, Jason. I want you in my class. But no hurting other children!" He listened impassively. If there were tears, he hid them behind lifeless, dry eyes.

Children who fail to develop compassion by the time they reach kindergarten are at risk to become sociopaths: hollow, dispassionate people without a conscience. Where lively emotion ought to exist there is only emotional dead space. Sociopaths are motivated only by self-interest. They have no empathy for others, although they might pretend sincerity to achieve self-gain. Their conscience is on permanent vacation. Sociopaths are broken souls isolated from caring by indifference and self-gratification. Was Jason becoming a broken soul?

Children are not born with a heart of cold marble. Healthy children arrive in the world with a rich capacity for emotional life. Anger, sadness, fear, and joy combine to create an emotional symphony that enables them to engage with others in a dance of compassion. They need partners to learn to share emotional experiences.

Resonate to children's emotions

To love a child is to share the child's experience. Showing this empathy is called "attunement." We can see attunement in the way loving parents talk with their children, the tone of their voices in response to their babies' coos, and the gentleness of their touches when their children long for contact. Infants respond to this emotional invitation to care by adjusting their attention and response to their parents' signals. Like two mirrors facing each other, their mutual reflection deepens the emotion being expressed.

In *The Interpersonal World of the Infant*, Daniel Stern refers to the emotions being shared in this way as "vitality affects."[5] The parent is not simply mimicking the specific emotions of the baby as much as their "flavor." On seeing the baby smile, the parent does not just smile back. The mother may widen her eyes and pull her head back slightly as she laughs and pats her baby's tummy. Then she says, "You're Mommy's baby! Yes you are!" The mother matches the tenor of her baby's experience and increases it by reflecting back a combination of sensory reactions similar to what her baby feels and is trying to tell her. Why is this reaction so powerful? The baby experiences an alignment with the mother, and a perfect emotional pitch is found by the resulting resonance.

Mighty Heart
Oliver Wood

Seventeen-year-old Oliver J. Wood rescued a thirty-nine-year-old man from a runaway truck in Madison, Ohio, on March 3, 2001. The man, a truck driver, had partially exited his idling truck when it began to roll backward down a slight grade. With the door handle in one hand and the steering wheel with the other, he was being dragged with his legs underneath the truck. Oliver was at work in front of a store located on the same street about 250 feet away when he saw the runaway truck approach. As its speed reached about 20 mph., Oliver rushed to the driver's side of the truck, climbing past the helpless man into the cab, and then pressed the brake pedal with his hand, bringing the truck to a stop. The driver was hospitalized with severe skin abrasions. Oliver also sustained an abrasion and swelling to his knee, which he had struck against the truck while entering. Both recovered.[8]

Such attunement has a powerful impact on an infant's physiology. It activates the opiate systems of both partners. Elevated levels of beta-endorphins make the experience pleasurable, and children begin to instinctively synchronize their emotions with those they love. By synchronizing with their children's emotions, parents also structure playful interactions, regulate attention, facilitate the development of verbal dialogue, and promote the capacity for self-regulation.[6] This emotional resonance contributes to the coordination of infants' physiological rhythms.[7] As they grow older, children continue to benefit from attunement. The mere presence of a parent or a brief touch may reconfirm the devotion that enables them to thrive.

Attunement is a spontaneous and authentic gift, a transformation of caring we discussed at Step Two (From Community to Caring).

Use "emotion" words

Talking about emotions to build children's emotional vocabulary is important for both compassion and insight. At about eighteen months parents begin using an emotional lexicon when referring to their toddlers' experiences. For example, during playtime, a father tells his son, "Danny, you're so happy!" Not long afterward, children begin using emotional language themselves. A three-year-old, for example, points to a crying child. With tears in his eyes, he tells his mother, "Oh, look. Baby is *sad.*" This child has learned that he can translate emotional experience into words.

When I taught preschool, I discovered that many of my four-year olds did not understand words like *sad, angry*, or *afraid*. They never heard these words used in the correct context. By three years, children should be able to talk about their experiences of feeling good, happy, sad, afraid, angry, loving, mean, and surprised.[9] Three-year-olds can speak with intensity about their attitudes and emotions.[10]

"My kitty gone—I cried."

"Mommy, I love you!"

"I like this swing!"

"Daddy, don't get that movie. It's too scary."

Emotions pictures file
(preschool-elementary)

Begin collecting magazine photos of people that express different emotions (sad, happy, afraid, and angry). Organize them in a file folder. Glue them to identical sizes of heavy construction paper to make them easier to handle and store. Collect at least three photo samples of each of the emotions described above.

Use the photos as flash cards. First, hold up one of the photos and ask your child *how* this person feels. If he does not know, tell him. Ask him to talk about *what* he thinks the causes of the happy, sad, afraid, or angry feelings might have been.

Second, mix up a stack of at least three pictures of each emotion in front of your child and ask him to group all the sad, happy, afraid, and angry faces together.

Third, show your child three pictures revealing a similar emotion and one that is clearly different and ask him to find the person who feels something different from the other three. Ask your child to explain.

Finally, ask your child to choose any three pictures from the collection. Then ask him to make up a story using the pictures. He can tell you the story or write it down.

By the age of six, children begin to understand the subtleties of different shades of the same emotion. Over 75 percent of six-year-olds will use words to describe feeling comfortable, excited, upset, glad, unhappy, relaxed, bored, annoyed, disappointed, shy, pleased, worried, calm, embarrassed, hating, nervous, and cheerful.[11]

We teach children an emotional vocabulary in three ways:

- By using the correct emotional terms to refer to our experience, e.g., "Jason, I feel very *sad*."

- By using the correct emotion terms to describe what we think our children feel, e.g., "Sally, you fell down and skinned your knee! Are you feeling *sad*?"

- By reading picture books or telling children stories that use emotion words, e.g., *Brave Irene* by William Steig.

As children begin to learn words for the basic emotions, we can contribute to their emotional vocabulary by talking about our feelings in two ways:

- By using imagery or metaphor for how we feel, e.g., "I feel as grouchy as a sick bear" or "I feel as angry as a hornet."

- By referring to the behavior the emotion prompts, e.g., "I feel like singing!" or "I feel like having a temper tantrum."

Children will learn to describe their inner world of emotion by hearing us put our experiences into words. During the late preschool years, children may begin using these more "poetic" forms of describing feelings. My four-year-old son once described his sadness by saying, "My heart feels like peanut butter."

Unfortunately, we have rituals in our society that impede the honest expression of emotions. Shortly after he arrived at preschool, I approached four-year-old Stephen to see why he was crying. I crouched at his eye level and asked, "Oh Stephen, how do you feel right now?" Between huge gasping sobs, he replied "I feel *fine!*" Even at his young age, he had learned to hide behind an impersonal exchange that is often part of our ritual of greeting.

The ability to recognize and put emotional experiences into words contributes to composure described in the previous chapter. Talking engages thinking parts of the brain that may shift experience from emotional arousal to thoughtful reflection.

Focus children's attention on the emotions of others

Although focusing on children's emotions is important, we can also invite them to shift their attention to the emotional lives of others. Not only can we talk about our emotions, we can point out what others may need and feel. For example, a mother and her toddler might see a child in a park begin to cry when his ice cream falls to the ground. The mother tells her little boy, "Oh look! See the baby crying! He's *sad* because his ice cream fell on the ground."

Research shows that discussions with older siblings about a newborn's feelings and needs have long-term positive consequences. In comparison to children who were not involved in these discussions, the older children were more affectionate toward the babies and were more likely to provide help. Three years later, they were more likely to share toys or candy with them. They were also more likely to comfort younger brothers or sisters who were distressed.[12]

Insight grows out of the discovery that other people have their own thoughts, values, and feelings. Very young children are primarily egocentric, unable to grasp what another person is thinking or to look at the world through another person's eyes. When four-year-old Sandy climbs the jungle gym in her party dress, she thinks nothing of swinging upside down with the dress over her head. She cannot see herself through the eyes of onlookers. Three years later, she would be horrified if she did this. At seven years old, she is capable of embarrassment because she can imagine what others are thinking of her.

The little lonely star
(preschool)

Put a cutting knife and apple out of sight while you talk with your child. Ask him if he knows what it means to be lonely. Then in your own words tell this story I created to talk with children about loneliness and sharing.

Once upon a time the sky was very dark at night. There were no stars . . . except one . . . a tiny star. This little star was all alone and felt lonely. One day, this little lonely star went to see a wise, old man who lived high on a mountain, as high to the stars as one could get. The little lonely star asked the old man if he could help. Because this old man loved the little star very much, and because he was wise and powerful, he said he would do two things. The old man reached behind him and pulled out a beautiful, shiny black bag. He opened it up, reached in and pulled out a handful of shimmering, glimmering stars. With one great swoop of his hand, he filled the night sky with thousands of other stars. The wise old man told the little star that now he would share the sky with many new friends. Then he said he would do something else to remind everyone on earth about the little star's importance. He would place the little star's image inside something special on earth.

Ask your child to guess where the old man put
the image of little star. Take out the apple and
carefully cut it through the center horizontally.
Pull the two halves back to reveal a star
shape inside. Now you both have a snack to
share.

Imagine blindfolding yourself and asking your
three-year-old to lead you around the house or
outdoors. Since three-year-olds cannot look at the
world through our eyes, they don't know how to
navigate us around obstacles that are unproblematic
for them, such as a tree branch under which they can
walk, but we cannot. A six-year-old would be more
capable of vigilance on our behalf.

Even so, what three-year-olds begin to learn about
emotions is impressive. When three- and four-year-
olds talked with their mothers about infant emotions as
expressed in photos they did more than comment
about the pictures ("He's crying"). They used emotion
words to explain causes ("He's happy because he likes
his mom"), to infer consequences ("If you were sad, I
would ask Daddy to hug you"), to obtain additional
information ("He's crying. What's wrong?"), and to
suggest solutions ("He's sad 'cause he needs his
mommy").[13]

At age four, children understood that the same
situation can give rise to different emotions in different
people. By age five, children can interpret emotions in
adult strangers' vocal tones and distinguish between
different emotional tones in infant vocalizations.[14] At
six, they can understand that the intensity of an
emotion can diminish over time.

The seven-year-old son of the owner of a local cafe occasionally stopped to talk with me when I was a customer. During one of our visits, we took turns drawing a picture together. He suddenly stopped his drawing to ask me seriously, "What's on your mind?" He really wanted to know what I was thinking at that exact moment. I described as simply as I could what I was thinking. He seemed satisfied with my answer and continued drawing. Six months earlier he would have been incapable of this question. He had made the incredible discovery that all people have their own private thoughts and feelings.

Forming relationships depends on sharing personal experiences. As our circles of self approach one another, boundaries exist where each of us stop and the other begins. How well we get to know each other in a relationship depends on the thickness of those boundaries. At first, infants have no boundaries—no knowledge of where they stop and others begin. They have no sense of self; no way to differentiate between themselves and others. When they hear another baby crying, they may begin crying too, aroused by the distress they may think is their own.

With experience, preschool children make the discovery of self. If we put a spot of rouge on a two-year-old child's nose, she will try to remove it when she sees herself in a mirror. She recognizes herself in the mirror and also realizes something is wrong. As children develop a sense of self, they begin to experience and label what they feel. Because their boundaries are essentially open, preschool children freely express their emotions and are readily affected by the emotions of others.

Allow children to experience spontaneous feelings of compassion

When my daughter was fourteen years old, I took her to Chicago to see *Les Misérables*. Shortly after arriving at our hotel, we went for a walk down the "Magnificent Mile," a street known for its luxury department stores. In addition to the wealthy elite, the area also attracted panhandlers and a high number of mentally ill street people. What I thought would be a fun afternoon of window-shopping turned into a drama worthy of a Greek tragedy.

I noticed right away the extremes of poverty and wealth that walked the street. My daughter, however, responded on a much deeper, emotional level. Growing up in a small Kansas town did not prepare her for the distress she felt emanating from so many people. The experience was so upsetting that she fled in tears. She could not bear to see such misery embedded in the glitter of wealth. Worse, well-groomed men in expensive suits and women draped in furs seemed to pretend the misery around them did not exist. The collision of desperation with indifference sent shock waves through her heart.

I could have been more supportive. Maybe I was in too intent to have a fun time with her. A heart touched by suffering deserves to be honored.

Show children how to be empathic

One morning I visited a public school to provide an in-service for teachers on self-esteem. The principal met me at the door and told me that one of the most popular children at the school had died the previous evening after becoming trapped in a freezer in an abandoned apartment. None of the teachers who were attending the training knew about the tragedy.

Instead of offering the intended program, I met with the teachers about gathering as a community to manage their grief so they could support the sad and frightened children who would arrive at school the next day. Because of my interest in stories and storytelling, I encouraged them to huddle with their children away from their desks to discuss their experiences and memories related to their friend and classmate. As we talked about possible books to read, one of the teachers expressed concern about crying in front of the children.[15]

I emphasized that her children needed to know what she felt. Her classroom is a community that was touched by the loss. Her tears bore witness to the love she felt for the child who died. Her tears would also make crying an acceptable expression of grief. If she cried, she could show her children how to respond to grief by inviting them to gather together close to her and to each other. As long as she remained composed, her tears would be a tribute to the young boy's life and an opportunity for the children to see genuine emotion by their teacher.[16]

Young children may become agitated in the presence of someone who is suffering. Eighteen-month-old children may even hit another child who is crying.[17] They are not trying to hurt the child; they just don't know how to respond when emotionally aroused. Hitting may be the very first thing to come to mind. An understanding parent or teacher can say, "People are for hugging, not for hitting," while hugging the child who was crying and inviting the toddler to join in.

Children as young as one year of age can learn to respond empathically to others. Carolyn Zahn-Waxler, Marian Radke-Yarrow, and their colleagues at the National Institute of Mental Health asked family members of one-year-old children to pretend sadness by sobbing, pain by yelling "ouch," and distress by coughing or choking. The children responded to each of these stimuli by patting and hugging the sufferer or by rubbing the "hurt" spot. While the children's reactions were strongest when they were interacting with their mothers, they also exhibited empathy toward complete strangers during the exercise.[18]

An empathic two-year-old is likely to run to his mother and take her to help his friend who has fallen down and hurt himself. Three-year-olds, however, make a dramatic adjustment in their strategy for helping. Instead of seeking their own mother, they are likely to look for the hurt child's mother to respond to the incident. This remarkable shift is an early sign of insight that demonstrates a greater awareness of the unique needs and feelings of others.

Showing children how to respond empathically does not mean teaching them to say "I'm sorry!" in a ritualistic, phony manner. I saw preschoolers on numerous occasions hurt someone, look around to see me watching, and then turn to those they hurt to say, "I'm sorry!" They didn't feel sorry. Their statement was a false incantation to escape my disapproval. They had learned that the words "I'm sorry" gave them wriggle room to avoid facing the consequences of a harmful choice.

Contrast this behavior with that of sweet and melancholy Stephen. One afternoon I was feeling unwell and getting sicker by the moment. As I sat in the back of the preschool waiting for all my children to leave, Stephen sat down next to me. I said, "Stephen, I feel really sick, really yucky right now." Stephen got up and put his arm around me. He looked at me with his sad, serious eyes and said with utmost sincerity, "Dokker Smith, you go home and your mommy take care of you."

A world without compassion would be frozen by indifference—a wintry landscape inhabited by isolated fortresses of self. Empathy brings the circles of our lives together and reminds us that we are not alone. Power, caring, vigilance, and composure are the primary ingredients for courage. With empathy, courage acts not by leaving the self behind but by bringing another person closer to our hearts. Letting oneself feel the suffering of others and see the world through their eyes are essential elements of the heroic spirit.

Step Six

From Morality
to Integrity

Keywords:
guidance, values, conventions,
moral rules, consistency, authority,
expectations, truth, fairness, faith,
conscience

Emphasis:
Act consistently with your
principles.

Tae kwon do athletes Esther Kim and Kay Poe had been friends since they began competing against each other as children. In 2000, Kay was considered to be America's best hope for an Olympic medal at Sydney.

Esther wasn't very far behind her friend. At the Olympic trials in Colorado, the two faced each other in a preliminary match. Kay won.

Still, Esther persevered and made her way through the qualifying rounds to gain a berth in the finals. She assumed she would meet Kay again.

Unfortunately, Kay dislocated her knee during an intense match just prior to the finals. Kay made eye contact with Esther after falling painfully to the mat. As tears streamed down her face, she shook her head in frustration as if to acknowledge that her dream had just shattered. Esther shouted encouragement from the sidelines. Kay then found the courage to rise from the ground to continue the match. Despite the painful injury, she won to advance to meet Esther in the finals. The winner would fulfill a lifelong ambition of competing at the Olympics.

But the injury was as bad as Kay suspected. Esther knew that Kay was in no shape to beat her and that she would likely defeat her injured friend and qualify for the Olympic team. She also knew that Kay was the better tae kwon do athlete and could easily be healthy by the time the Olympic Games began. Esther wondered what kind of honor would there really be in such a victory?

Before the match, Esther approached her friend. Kay was lying on the floor, crying. She looked up at Esther and said, "We are going to fight; we are going to fight." Esther responded, "How are you going to fight—you can't even stand up. You know it's not fair for me to walk into the ring having two legs, and you have one leg and fighting you."

Esther was also scared. What if during the match she struck a blow that would permanently damage Kay's knee?

Esther made a decision. She told Kay, "Let me bow out to you. Please don't argue with me; please just accept it because I want this."

Esther officially withdrew from the match and gave her injured friend the victory and the Olympic berth. The referee raised Kay's hand and Kay raised Esther's hand and the two embraced in tears.

Esther's decision was remarkable, revealing a true heart of honor and good sportsmanship. She made the choice of integrity. She acted consistently with her guiding principles of fairness. Although Kay Poe failed to win a medal at the Sydney Games, she and Esther had demonstrated to a cynical world that courage, integrity, and sacrifice are more important than personal gain.

The importance of integrity

Integrity means acting consistently with a personal standard of behavior. This code serves as a moral compass that provides clear direction amid conflict and confusion. Those with integrity have learned principles that guide their lives. Those without integrity are unsure of how to respond to difficult situations, and are lacking an important aspect of the sense of self.

When I asked a group of children in one of my storytelling concerts to define courage, a third grader eagerly waved her hand. When I called on her, she replied, "Courage is doing what you know is right!" Certainly, Kay Poe chose to do what she knew was right. Chris Haney (see page 145) also did what he knew was right when he shimmied up a towering pine tree to carry the ten-year-old to safety. They both acted with integrity.

Interviews with heroic rescuers of Jews during World War II and Carnegie Hero Medal recipients revealed two common traits: First, they were uncomfortable with others referring to them as "heroes." They argued that they did only what any decent person would do. They believed they did not really deserve praise. How could anyone single out such a natural act as special? Eva Fogelman writes, "Moral rescuers . . . when asked why they risked their lives to aid Jews, often answered, 'How else should one react when a human life is endangered?' Their concept of right and wrong was so much a part of who they were and are, that it was as if I had asked them why they breathed."[1]

Second, the heroic rescuers shared a powerful underlying respect for *all* human life and a strong sense of personal and social responsibility for others. Eva Fogelman found that the acceptance of people who are different was an early emotional touchstone in rescuers' integrity. "From the earliest ages, rescuers were taught by their parents that people are inextricably linked to one another. No one person or group was better than any other was. The conviction that all people, no matter how marginal, are of equal value was conveyed to children of both religious and nonreligious households."[2]

Because of this conviction, racist propaganda had no effect on them. When life is cherished, those who value it react as Amanda Valance did when she stayed behind in the Orlando canal to rescue her friend Edna from an alligator: "For a split second, I felt like I had to

Mighty Heart
Chris Haney

Ten-year-old Chris Haney was eating lunch in his backyard on July 21, 2001, in Lincolnton, North Carolina, when he heard screams for help in a neighbor's yard. He raced next door where he saw a ten-year-old girl dangling upside down, clinging to a spindly branch of a pine tree nearly thirty feet overhead.

The girl's grandmother screamed for her to hold on while the other children ran to get help. Chris decided there was no time to wait for an adult to respond. Wearing nothing but cutoff shorts, Chris scrambled up the poison-ivy-covered tree to the child's side. He told her to wrap her arms around his neck.

She had to hold on with her elbows because of her burned hands. Chris did not know that a high-voltage power line had shocked the ten-year-old while she was climbing, severely burning more than a fifth of her body. (Emergency workers later compared the shock from the 7,200-volt line to a lightning strike.)

Chris told her, "Whatever you do, don't let go of me. Don't worry. It's going to be all right." Later Chris recalled, "I don't know if she said anything—but if she did, I couldn't understand her because she was crying."

Chris slipped a little as he descended. It took all the tenacity possible of a 100-pound boy to carry a 60-pound girl while descending. As he lowered her from limb to limb, he pinned her legs against his stomach so she wouldn't fall.

Chris was shaking as he brought the girl to the ground. Sweat soaked his hair. The girl had third-degree burns on her shoulders, hands, legs and feet. Her hair and clothes were burned. An ambulance rushed her to the hospital where she recovered.

Her father said, "Without (Chris), she probably would have fallen and broke her neck." Chris said he was thinking only about the girl. "I was happy that I got her down, but I was scared she was going to die." His mother added, "He doesn't think it was such a big deal . . . But we definitely know different."[3]

leave, but *I could not do that to her.*" As John Cerqueira helped bring a woman in a wheelchair down seventy flights of stairs at the World Trade Center he heard his mother's voice warning him to get out of the building. *"But I had to help"* was his response. There was a moral imperative underlying their actions. Self-respect demanded that they remain true to themselves. They risked their lives to save others because their consciences demanded they act.

Discovery of autonomous morality

The clear sense of right and wrong shown by those who display either sudden or persistent courage is an example of what Jean Piaget called an "autonomous morality." Before elementary school, children derive their moral principles from authority, represented by their parents. What is right and wrong is what Mommy and Daddy say is right and wrong. Children do not yet have the intellectual capacity to make independent judgments. To be a good person, they reason, is to obey adult authority. This orientation is what psychologists call an *external locus of control*. They look for direction outside of themselves.

As their brains mature, children become more thoughtful. During the elementary school years, they begin to think for themselves and to question standards they have been taught. They begin to design their own road map. If they choose to behave according to values they "own," they then have an *internal locus of control*.

An *external* locus of control is by its nature weak because the presence of authority is required for obedience. If the moral authority or reward is absent, children with an external locus of control are free to behave according to impulse. In contrast, an *internal* locus of control is integrated into one's personality, independent of any outside dominating force. Thirteen-year-old Camelio Torres (see page 151) took the initiative to rescue a two-year-old from a submerged car based on the imperative of an internal locus of control.

How would you respond?
(elementary)

Ask children to reflect on and assess their capacity for caring. Make up a story about each of the following situations to put the question into context. After creating the situation, ask your child,

What would you do . . .

- if you saw someone put a drug in someone's drink?

- if you heard someone make cruel and unfair statements about a child you did not know?

- if you saw someone deliberately push a smaller child down on the playground?

One can also be heroic on one's own behalf. Make up additional stories about several adversities related to the list below that your child might face and ask,

Would it bother you if . . .

- you stood up in class and forgot what you were going to say?

- someone blamed you for something you did not do?

- someone said mean things about you to other people?

There could be extenuating circumstances that would decrease the amount of anger, fear, or sadness a child might experience in these situations. As you listen to your children's comments, point out the underlying values your child expresses.

In a letter on a CNN Internet forum on the Columbine High School shooting, Bobbie Gogain wrote, "I do feel that there are many students today that feel no remorse for doing wrong things . . . somewhere, somehow, the feeling of what is right and wrong has gone from many of today's youth. I dealt with a student that stole three cars recently, and in the process of trying to understand . . . the why's of this situation, I asked the a student (a twelve-year-old sixth grade girl) if she did not hear an inner voice telling her that to steal was wrong. She looked at me and said, 'What inner voice? What are you talking about lady? I hear no inner voice.'"

Nurturing integrity

- **Distinguish between conventions and moral principles**
- **Invest emotion in moral principles**
- **Give spiritual depth to moral principles**
- **Act consistently with our values**
- **Establish reasonable limits to emphasize moral principles**

Children do not have to reject their parents' values in the process of acquiring an internal locus of control. Parents who remain lovingly engaged with their children will have a powerful, inspirational effect on the values their children choose to claim as their own. Demanding that children believe what we say and do what we want may achieve conformity to our wishes, but at the loss of their integrity. Morality cannot flourish when fear of reprisal enforces moral rules. If children remain locked into an external locus of control, their borrowed values are weak and short-lived. If we want our influence to endure, we have to let our children make choices. If we deprive them of opportunities to make moral choices, we rob them of independently won integrity. Courage and heroism are possible only with an *internal locus of control*.

In her study of heroic rescuers, Eva Fogelman discovered the power of loving parents for instilling integrity in their children at an early age:

It was not a whim that led these people to risk their lives and those of their families, but a response, almost a reflexive reaction in some cases, that came from core values developed and instilled in them in childhood. These childhood experiences and influences formed a leitmotif that played through the histories of most rescuers . . . a nurturing, loving home; an altruistic parent or beloved caretaker who served as a role model for altruistic behavior; a tolerance for people who were different; a childhood illness or personal loss that tested their resilience and exposed them to special care; and an upbringing that emphasized independence, competence, discipline with explanations (rather than physical punishment or withdrawal of love), and caring.[4]

Although every practice described in this book has an effect on integrity, the five described with this step have special significance.

Distinguish between conventions and moral principles

As they shape their beliefs about right and wrong, children differentiate between two types of rules: conventions and moral principles.

Conventions are the agreed-upon uniformities in social behavior, and are considered binding within the society honoring them. Another way to define conventions is "expectations related to cultural practices that regulate behavior." School rules, forms of address, expectations governing attire and appearance, game rules, family rules (e.g., saying grace), and customs (like the polite way to eat soup or spaghetti) are examples of conventions. Breaking a convention triggers disapproval. Conventions are arbitrary; they are neither permanent nor universal. The behaviors

Mighty Heart
Camelio Torres

Thirteen-year-old Camelio Torres helped to save a two-year-old cousin from drowning in Cuba, New Mexico, on April 28, 1990. The toddler was inside her family's sport and utility vehicle when it rolled into Dragonfly Lake and began to sink in twelve feet of water. Camelio jumped into the icy water with his clothes on, swam to the car, and reached it about twenty feet from the bank. He entered through the back door, crawled over the back seat, and seized the small child, maneuvering her through the rear door and out of the car. A nearby fisherman also swam to the vehicle and helped bring the child to the bank. Within moments of the rescue, the vehicle was completely submerged.[5]

they regulate have no inherent damaging interpersonal effects, other than a possible disruption of social order.[6] Someone in authority can change a convention.

Moral principles are similar to conventions in that they are also rules that govern behavior. Moral principles, however, relate to universal and timeless needs of individuals and communities. Unlike conventions, public opinion cannot undermine the importance of moral principles. Despite differences between cultures in table manners, for example, every society attaches significance to the value of human life. Universal moral principles address physical and psychological harm, health and well-being, fairness and rights, and such positive prosocial moral behaviors as sharing and helping.[7]

A personal coat of arms
(elementary)

 Set out crayons, colored pencils, or marking pens and a large sheet of construction paper or poster board, cut to a size that would fit on a child's bedroom door.

Draw a large shield on the paper. Draw a vertical and horizontal line dividing the shield into approximately four equal parts.

Explain to your child, if necessary, that a coat of arms is a shield that depicts symbols of a family's ancestry. Set out another blank coat of arms for yourself so you can work simultaneously alongside your child.

> In the top left-hand quadrant, draw something that frightens you. In the adjacent quadrant, draw a picture of confronting the fear.
>
> In the bottom left quadrant, draw a picture of doing something kind for another family member. In the right, draw a picture of doing something kind for someone outside of the family.
>
> While you draw, talk with your child about the actions each of you chose to illustrate. Tape the coats of arms to each of your bedroom doors or walls. If there is enough room, tape the drawings on the same wall.

Children learn at an early age to draw distinctions between what is wrong only when there are rules against it (conventions) and acts that are always wrong (moral principles). Wearing a bathrobe to school, going into the opposite sex's bathroom, cracking your knuckles, or playing with your food oppose most conventions and may get a person into trouble with the authorities but do not deserve severe sanctions. These offenses are not immoral. On the other hand, even young children who have a healthy conscience regard breaking a promise, stealing flowers, kicking a harmless animal, and destroying another's property as inherently wrong.[8]

Moral principles can be *affirmative* or *prohibitive*. Affirmative principles prescribe action, for example, "intervene on behalf of a victim" or "help someone who has fallen down." Affirmative principles are effective because they teach children *what to do*. Telling a child to "solve your problems with words" is affirmative. A prohibitive message like "Stop hitting!" emphasizes *what not to do* and fails to teach a way to handle a situation. In practice, both types of principles work together. For example, a father may tell his young teen to refrain from swearing while patiently demonstrating how to communicate his anger properly. "Do this, not that" is the most effective type of teaching message.

Children can be aware of standards on prohibited behavior by age three. By the end of kindergarten, children should be using internalized rules, strategies, and plans to regulate their behavior and be kind to others, even though they may not always be aware of the underlying morality.[9] The Utku Eskimo of Hudson Bay call this awareness *ihuma* (translated as "reason"); the Fijians call it *vakayalo* ("sense of what is proper").

Research shows that peers are often the most powerful advocates for moral principles. Adults typically insist that children conform to social conventions just as often as they press for obedience to moral rules. Many parents, for example, often become equally or more upset when a child spills his milk as when he hits his younger brother. In contrast, moral violations are much more upsetting to children than conventional violations.[10] Children generally do not care about things that often upset adults, e.g., eating with their fingers, talking too loud, or going to bed with dirty feet. They do care, though, if their brother or sister hits them, tears up their homework, or takes something that belongs to them.

Children react emotionally to these moral transgressions by retaliating against offenders. Young children might tell a peer who pushes them down, "I'm not going to invite you to my birthday party!" The disapproval of peers and siblings can have a significant influence in shaping behavior. While parents often fail to distinguish clearly between the conventional and the moral, children reserve their greatest emotional disapproval for the moral failure of their peers.

Our messages will be more influential if we emphasize the priority of moral action over conventional conformity—that is, responding more strongly to our children's mistreatment of others than to leaving dirty clothes on the floor. We can look for and emphasize moral principles that might lie *beneath* a convention, for example, "Pick up toys because someone might trip and get hurt."

Invest emotion in moral principles

Violations of moral principles deserve an emotional response that marks the offense as significant. We should reserve our greatest disgust, anger, and sorrow for moral failure. If an emotional reaction is absent, then the violation becomes arbitrary and less binding, merely a conventional breach.

Integrity in action
(late preschool-elementary)

Demonstrate for your children that values are meant to be put into action. Consider participating in any of the following activities:

Ask your children to choose some of their toys to take to a homeless shelter (and bring some things of your own). Alternatively, if they have money saved from allowances, shop for something new to donate.

Clean up a playground area at a local park.

Volunteer to distribute food at a food bank.

Volunteer with your older children to help prepare and distribute food at a soup kitchen.

Contact the United Way in your community to learn about volunteer opportunities that can involve your family. If possible, choose something based on a concern or interest of your children. For example, if your children are attracted to animals, volunteer with them at a local animal shelter or zoo. Make a commitment of about once a week over a reasonable length of time if possible. Invite young children to keep track of the experience by painting or drawing pictures of what takes place. Older children and their parents can keep a journal.

Integrity is more than an intellectual commitment to ideas of right and wrong. Integrity is also emotional and passionate. Moral principles have to be a part of someone from the neck down, an "in the bones" thing; that is, in every fiber of a person's being. That's why courageous rescuers feel the attention they receive is unjustified. What they did was the result of values they had woven into the fabric of their lives. They believed responding courageously was the normal thing to do. They had a clear sense of right and wrong and they stood up for their beliefs. They had independent minds and never simply followed the crowd.[11]

Children need to see our passion for important things. Parents who were sad and disappointed when using victim-centered explanations of their discipline (e.g., "See, you hurt Paula! Be gentle; don't push others down!") more effectively communicated to their children the inherent wrong in their actions than parents who showed no emotion or simply prohibited the behavior.[12]

What makes television violence so harmful is not the violence itself, but the reaction of parents who show indifference to the misery portrayed. If we don't react passionately to the violence, we send a message to children that violence is more an issue of convention than morality. Violent programs on television are damaging, not because of the programs themselves but because of the attitude of casual acceptance of violence by adults who watch them with children. As James Claxton points out in his book *Wise Up*, "They learn by observation that their natural revulsion or fear is unnecessary, or, worse, is 'stupid' or 'babyish' so they become numbed down as well as dumbed down by the experience."[13]

Give spiritual depth to moral principles

Every courageous act, every example of heroism, whether it is sudden and unexpected or persistent over a long term, is essentially spiritual. Fundamental principles may motivate the act, but the spiritual power of hope keeps courage alive. The parent who gets up every night to care for a severely ill child or the single mother who goes to a difficult job every day to provide for her young children may do so out of hope that her sacrifice will make a better life for her children. Hope is inspiration for children who take a deep breath either in a confrontation with a bully or in a struggle with asthma.

Hope is a companion to faith. Hope and faith are both spiritual elements in courage because they operate from more than logic. Hope and faith lead to a conviction that a course of action has ultimate worth and that some good can result from taking the risk inherent in the action. The passengers on United Flight 93 who rose up against their captors may have concluded that their horrible ordeal would have a tragic outcome. Nevertheless, hope put the outcome in some doubt. Faith in their ability to act gave them hope that their uprising would prevent more tragedy. Their courage had meaning.

While hope and faith are often involved in the ability to take a risk or endure a sacrifice, this spiritual component of courage does not necessarily have religious implications. Bert Bochove, a Dutch rescuer of Jews during World War II, said, "My feeling when doing it [saving Jews] was that it had nothing to do with religion. If I was not a Christian, I would still do it. You have it in you."[14] Another rescuer, whose father was a minister, was on the Gestapo's "most wanted" list because he organized and operated an escape route to take Jews to Switzerland and Spain. He was a devout Seventh Day Adventist whose life was permeated by religion. Yet even he said, "I don't think you had to be religious. You had to have love in your heart."[15] The moral principle of the sanctity of human life transcends religion.

While not overtly religious, the concept of sanctity is essentially spiritual. We don't take a courageous stand or make a sacrifice purely out of logic. Logic may insist that we protect ourselves first, flee, or give up. When we act courageously, we resist "logic" because something outside of us beckons us to greatness. This *something* is transcendent and mystical.

We need to show this spiritual part of our lives to our children, no matter what our religious practices. We might watch a glorious sunset together, walk with them under the stars, or pray with them during a difficult time. Spiritual experiences invite children to contemplate greater powers that exist outside of the narrow confines of self. Every heroic act is an affirmation of something greater than self-interest.

Act consistently with our values

Remaining true to oneself can require courage. During my visit to a Kiwanis club in southeast Kansas, a father shared with the group how difficult it was for him to put his arm around his teenage daughter in public. He was afraid of public disapproval and let his fear control his behavior. We talked about how much his daughter needed those hugs, possibly more now than ever before. A public display of affection is a signal to others, especially predatory older males, that he both loves and protects his daughter. He may have told her a hundred times, even a *thousand* times how much he loves her, but actions always speak louder than words. Acting out of fear instead of principle undermines his daughter's respect. She needs to find a source of courage in her father, whether in private or public.

Children learn by observing us. They are more likely to copy what we do than what we say. The father who spanks his son for hitting his sister sends an even more violent son off to school. When our behavior gives substance to our beliefs, then our children have a more powerful image to follow.

Establish reasonable limits to emphasize moral principles

A single mother approached me after a responsive discipline workshop. She told me she was having trouble with her fourteen-year-old daughter. Every night she insisted her daughter be home at a reasonable time. Every night the daughter said terrible things to her because of the restrictions. The continual conflict was exhausting. "She tells me every time that she would be happier with her friends." The mother sighed and turned her eyes to the floor. "Maybe I should just let her go." She was ready to give up.

I asked her if she knew her daughter's friends. She sighed, rolled her eyes, and nodded. "Are her friends happy?" I asked. She gazed again at the floor. When she looked up, she was smiling. "No, they are not really happy." I replied, "That's right. They are deeply unhappy because they don't have parents like you who are willing to stand up to them for what they believe is right." We talked some more about managing the struggles of raising her daughter alone. I hope she left feeling stronger and more confident.

Our children need us to be their heroes. What does that mean, practically? They want us to stand up for our beliefs and to show that we have the courage of our convictions. Think of one of your children. Imagine this child at fifty years old, and then ask him or her, "What did your mom (or dad) teach you while you were growing up? What about you is true because she and no other was your mom? What difference did she make?" How would you want your child to respond? Do your discipline practices contribute to this outcome?

Although children need parents willing to exercise the responsibilities of authority, they *don't* want parents bludgeoning them with their beliefs. The ability to think and act independently is a crucial life skill, and a key element in rescue activity. Eva Fogelman observed that

> Coming to the aid of a persecuted people required an independent mind. A person had to be accustomed to reasoning through a problem and coming to a conclusion not based on what others thought or what the laws mandated. Those raised in authoritarian families were not likely to resist the pressure to conform. However, not all rescuers were raised in lenient, democratic homes. . . . This kind of strict discipline, however, did not crush the self. On the contrary, rescuers' families nourished an independence of mind and spirit. They set direction, lent support, and then sent the children out on their own.[16]

Samuel and Pearl Oliner discovered that those who rescued Jews during World War II used reasoning as discipline more than did the parents of nonrescuers.[17]

As parents, we are the champions for the next generation, with the obligation to use our devotion and courage to give our children character. Our greatest gift to our children is neither money, nor property, nor fame. Our most powerful parental legacy is a heart and mind enriched by the example of our lives. Long after we are gone, the integrity we revealed to our children will continue to be a source of courage for those who made it a part of themselves. Like Olympic hopeful Esther Kim, they will take their place of honor by acting in harmony with their convictions.

Step Seven

From Justice
to Honor

Keywords:
responsibility, duty, accountability,
fairness, forgiveness, consequences
and alternatives thinking,
guilt and shame, personal cost,
excuses, bargaining, loss of face,
lying, pride

Emphasis:
Take responsibility
for your behavior.

On Friday night, January 11, 2002, five teenage girls stood before a packed gymnasium at Danville High School (Vermont) just before the start of the varsity game. Although the five girls were members of the Danville High School basketball team (four were starters), they were not in uniform. They were there to explain to the community why their coach had kicked them off the team.

Coach Tammy Rainville had a zero-tolerance rule on drugs and alcohol for members of her team. All the girls who played for her knew about her policy, but the five girls who stood on the gym floor that night had broken the rules. The five girls drank alcohol at a New Year's Eve party, and when classes resumed after the holiday break, stories about these parties began to circulate. As a group, they decided to tell Coach Rainville the full story before the rumor mill made things even worse.

The coach told them she could not back down on her policy. The players, two juniors and three seniors, understood and agreed. Their standing together that Friday night in the gym was their public demonstration of support of the coach's decision. They had another message too. They wanted to call attention to a problem in their community.

One of the seniors spoke last. "We hope you will understand that we are not bad kids. We made a mistake. What we did was definitely not worth it. We hope this event will make everyone open their eyes and realize that there is a big drug and alcohol problem in our community. And if you work with us to try to solve this problem, you will help us feel that we have not been thrown off our basketball team for nothing."

The five left the floor to deafening applause. That night a large crowd saw five teenagers approach the microphone and witnessed five young adults leave.[1] Not only did they have integrity, these young women were committed to act honorably. They didn't demand special treatment as athletes or find lawyers to sue the coach to force reinstatement. They made the decision that duty, responsibility, and honor were more important than personal gain or athletic glory.

Honor, responsibility, and accountability

Honor is a choice to accept responsibility for acting with integrity while under duress. Honor is a test of commitment to our beliefs of right and wrong. Chris Haney displayed honor when he scurried up a tree to rescue a burned child. Camelio Torres passed the test of honor when he rescued a two-year-old from a submerged vehicle. The Danville girls accepted the consequences of their choice to ignore the agreement with their coach.

Common examples of honor that occur during childhood include:

- An eight-year-old breaks a neighbor's window while playing baseball. She goes to the neighbor's house and tells him she was responsible.

- A ten-year-old resists his mother's offers to help on a difficult school project and insists on doing all the work himself.

- A fourteen-year-old tells the teenage driver of a car in which she is riding that she wants to go home after the group stops to purchase beer and decides to go to a park to drink.

Likewise, Shawn Durrant (see page 167) did not stand idly by when a five-year-old was in grave danger. He took his responsibility as the operator of the ski lift seriously and his responded to the test of honor. In each case, young people made a choice to act out of conviction.

Such honor is a critical element in courage and heroism. Those without honor do not intervene on behalf of others because they assume somebody else will take responsibility for acting with integrity when others are in danger. If an irresponsible choice causes unpleasant consequences, they point fingers to something or someone else to avoid accountability. Culture and cinema critic Roger Ebert spotlighted this widespread flight from responsibility when he observed, "We live in an age when tragedy does not have heroes, only victims." The events of September 11, 2001, provided us with many examples of heroism embedded in tragedy and demonstrated that such an indictment is not universally true.

Among families who risked everything to rescue Jews during World War II, some young people's sense of honor propelled them to go beyond their parents' own efforts. For example, sixteen-year-old Antosia Adamowicz was ordinarily a dutiful Lithuanian daughter. One night she could not sleep, knowing that four Jews were freezing in a ditch on her family's Lithuanian farm. Her parents had forbidden her to go out into the snowstorm, but Antosia knew that the shivering Jews had not eaten in two days and would die without food. Antosia decided to disobey her parents. She found a loaf of bread and a kettle of water and left her home to find the starving family. She went barefoot, brushing clean the footprints behind her as she trudged through the deep snow left by the storm. The food she brought saved four lives.[2]

Mighty Heart
Shawn Durrant

On January 29, 1990, eighteen-year-old Shawn Durrant helped save a five-year-old from falling from a Liberty, Utah, ski lift. Thirty feet above the hard-packed snow, the child had slipped from the seat and was dangling from the grasp of her mother. Unable to lift her child back into the chair, the mother screamed for help. Shawn was one of the lift's operators. He immediately instructed the other operator to advance the chair to the nearest support. Shawn scaled the forty-foot tower and walked across the narrow, unprotected crossbeam to the point at which the lift's cable was secured. The chair was just beyond his reach, so he jumped from the beam to grasp the cable. Shawn moved hand-over-hand to the chair connection and slid down into the chair beside the mother. He then reached down, grasped the five-year-old, and helped her mother pull the girl back into the seat. The lift was restarted, and they rode, uninjured, to safety.[3]

Nurturing honor

Children want to respect their parents. However, we have to earn our children's respect by meeting the test of responsibility. When we establish firm and reasonable limits to protect and guide our children, we must stand by our beliefs and enforce them with reasonable but firm consequences. Do we have the grit to stand up for what we believe is important? On the other hand, will we avoid confrontation by being too permissive or by making idle threats? Integrity that is fragile and easily abandoned under pressure does not earn respect.

Demonstrate responsibility

- **Demonstrate responsibility**
- **Teach consequences and alternatives thinking**
- **Hold children accountable for their actions**
- **Talk with children about justice**
- **Use shame and guilt cautiously**

At one time, my son was a police officer who worked nights in a rough urban neighborhood. He and his partner responded to an obscene 911 call. The 911 operator directed them to a pay phone near a large apartment complex. When they arrived, they were shocked to find a five-year-old girl on the phone. The two officers talked to the child about the dangers of making a careless call on an emergency line. She promised not to repeat the misbehavior. The officers left the area shaking their heads and feeling disturbed by the absence of parental guidance and supervision.

Shortly afterward, they received a second alert from their dispatcher about another obscene 911 call from the same phone. They returned to the telephone booth. The same child ran away when she saw them approach. My son and his partner left their car and followed the child on foot to her apartment. The child's mother answered their knock on the door. When they explained what the young girl had done, the mother became abusive, screaming about police "harassment." The officers informed the mother that the phone company would remove the public phone booth if her daughter repeated the obscene 911 calls. Since many of the residents depended on this booth for access to a telephone, the loss would be a setback for all of the families living in the complex.

Contrast this response to the actions of another mother. A woman who attended one of my discipline workshops told me that she had recently received a call from her son's seventh grade teacher.[4] He was goofing off in class, distracting students, and upsetting classroom order. He was the class clown and enjoyed being the center of attention. The teacher and his mother had talked about his disruptive behavior on several occasions. At this point, the teacher was ready to give up and remove the boy from the class. After further discussion, the mother and teacher decided to make one more try.

When her son arrived home from class, his mother said to him:

> I have talked to Mrs. Martin about your behavior in her class. You are a smart and capable child and your disruptive behavior will stop. How you have chosen to act in class is making life difficult for the teacher and interfering with other

students' learning. I have also talked to my boss, and he has agreed to help. Tomorrow, when you enter Mrs. Martin's classroom, you will see an empty desk at the back of the room. If you misbehave, the next day when you enter the class you will see me sitting in that desk. I will remain there every class meeting until you stop your disruptive behavior. Now it's up to you.

The teacher called the following evening. She was amazed. The boy had made a complete reversal in his misbehavior.

His mother's strategy worked for three reasons. First, her son knew her word mattered. His mother never made an idle threat. He knew she would be there, in that chair, if he misbehaved. He knew she would remain in the chair until his disruptive behavior stopped. He would receive no reprieve from the consequences, no second chance. Second, her decision was an expression of love because it required her to sacrifice time and effort on his behalf. Third, she affirmed his underlying intelligence and self-control. Since he had chosen to be the class clown, he could choose to stop.

The mother demonstrated honor in the exercise of responsibility. She acted reasonably according to a principle of fairness. She understood and accepted the consequences of her choice. She did not need to reprimand, spank, or take privileges away from her child. She was willing to accept accountability as a parent. She was a "hands-on parent," willing to stay engaged in her son's life.

Teach consequences and alternatives thinking

Honor is based on knowing that alternatives are available, and making a choice knowing the potential consequences. Preschool children can learn that their behavior is a choice that has consequences for others.[5] One day Steven, a four-year-old in my preschool class, approached me and gently grabbed my beard. "Does this hurt?" he asked. "No," I said. Then he pulled a little harder and repeated the question. "Does *this* hurt?" "No," I said. After the third firm tug I replied, "That's starting to hurt Steven, but just a little." That answer appeared to satisfy his curiosity. He replied, "OK!" and then went to play with his friends.

Why did he pull my beard? At some point, his parents may have insisted, "Stop pulling your sister's hair. You're hurting her!" That statement could have got him thinking. He liked to run his fingers through my beard when I talked to him. He may have wondered whether he was hurting me when he did this. He tested the idea by performing an experiment with me. My reaction was reassuring and helped him better understand the consequences of his acts.

There are many classic stories that emphasize consequences of choices. King Midas paid the price when everything he touched turned to gold. Goldilocks discovered the consequences of meddling in the home of the Three Bears. Little Red Riding Hood suffered for not acting on her intuition when the wolf disguised himself as her grandmother.

The Mightiest Heart by Lynn Cullen (Dial Books for Young Readers, 1998) is a story about the painful consequences of misjudgment and the love that perseveres despite injustice. Based on a Welsh legend, the story recounts the sad trials of the faithful dog Gelert, the "Mightiest Heart." Gelert loves and is completely devoted to his master, Prince Llywelyn. Unfortunately, the Prince's mistrusting and jealous wife gradually undermines his trust in his faithful friend.

Llywelyn makes a tragic mistake when he blames Gelert for an attack on his baby, not realizing that the real predator was a wolf. Only after venting his rage does Llywelyn discover that Gelert actually saved his baby's life. By the time Llywelyn discovers the truth, Gelert has fled into the forest wilderness.

The distraught and guilt-ridden prince sets out to find Gelert to right his injustice. During his search deep in the forest, a wolf attacks him. Gelert suddenly arrives to defend his beloved master. Laurel Long's magnificent artwork perfectly captures the anguish of the moment as Llywelyn holds a victorious but exhausted and starving Gelert. After Llywelyn falls asleep, Gelert slips into the forest, leaving the prince to experience the enormity of his loss alone.

What happens next?
(elementary)

Create a list of events in which one thing has an effect on another. Begin with acts of nature. For example:

The air turns freezing cold over a lake.

Lightning hits a dry forest.

An egg falls out of a bird's nest.

Rain falls on wildflowers.

The sun shines on wet grass.

Then move to interpersonal effects. For example:

One child slaps another in the face.

A child slips and falls on the street.

A child receives a gift from a friend.

A child does not eat breakfast before going to school.

A child eats too much cake.

Make up more situations familiar to your child. After each situation, ask, "What might happen next?" The primary purpose of this activity is to encourage children to think playfully in terms of causes and effects, not to guess the "correct" answer.

Encouraging children to consider the alternatives to and consequences of their actions is a form of mindfulness. In addition to reading stories to help them be more aware of cause and effect, we can also challenge them to anticipate consequences. We might tell them:

"Use your brain."

"That's a great idea."

"What do you think will happen next?"

"What do you think of that?"

"Give me another idea."

"What did you see (hear, smell, taste, touch)?"

"What else could you do?"

When they do act, we can point out the consequences of their choices. For example, if we notice our child give a hug to a playmate who smiles in response, his father might say, "Jerry, it was nice of you to give Angela a hug. Look at her smile!" If a toddler slaps a playmate in frustration, her mother could respond with a sad face, "Tonya, don't hit Julia! Hitting hurts her and makes her sad. See her tears?" Before their third birthday, children can understand that their actions have consequences, good and bad, for others.

Hold children accountable for their actions

When our children do something harmful, we can emphasize the consequences by giving them something useful to do to demonstrate accountability. For example, we could tell Tonya to get a washcloth and gently wipe Julia's tear-stained face. Saying "I'm sorry" does not satisfy the demands of honor. We have to show regret by correcting the problem or demonstrating sincere remorse when we cannot.

Noble choices have their consequences as well. A mother of a teenage boy told me about the trouble her son encountered after breaking up a fight at school. The authorities punished him as well as those who started the fight. Her son was quite upset about the unfair treatment. This example points out that the choice of honor does not always have favorable results. The idea that everything will always turn out favorably if we do the right thing is a dangerous illusion. This

Mighty Heart
Annell Bings

On July 19, 1994, seventeen-year-old Annell Bings helped save a sixty-five year old woman from drowning when the car she was a passenger in went off the road near Mount Currie, British Columbia, into the Birkenhead River, sixty feet from the nearest bank. The car began to sink in eleven feet of frigid snowmelt water from the mountains and nearby ice fields.

Annell managed to open one of the car's rear doors, exit the vehicle, and swim to the bank. When she didn't see any other passengers escaping the car, she plunged back in, returned to the now-submerged car, and attempted to open the door. She entered the car partially, grasped the unconscious woman, and brought her to the surface. Annell swam to the bank with the helpless older woman, and managed to grasp one end of a rope thrown to her by a witness to the accident. With this additional help, Annell brought the woman to safety. Cold and tired, both recovered from effects of the ordeal, though the older woman required hospitalization. Another woman in the car also survived, but the driver drowned.[6]

boy made the choice to intervene. He stopped the fight. Now he has to endure the consequences of that choice, hopefully with some comfort from having behaved honorably.

Doing nothing is also a choice that can have unpleasant consequences. What if the bully landed one strong blow to the other person's head and killed him? An honorable person asks, "What is the right action for me to take right now in this difficult circumstance?" The young man evaluated the risks and chose to break up the fight before such an occurrence could happen because of his *internal locus of control*. That decision brought him into conflict with school authorities. There is an important lesson here: take responsibility and be accountable even when others do not recognize that motivation of honor.

Accountability means coming to terms with the price of integrity. Every act of courage involves hope and faith. Hope tells us that the best possible outcome *may* occur. Faith reassures us that we *can manage* what follows—even when the aftermath may be as difficult as the initial act of courage.

We hold children accountable because we hope they will learn to take responsibility for themselves. When they are very young, this means learning to obey authority figures. My son's kindergarten class was held in a building separate from the rest of the school. Just before the winter holiday, the school scheduled a festive half-day event. Soon after they arrived, he and his classmates lined up to walk over to the main building for the program. All the children were restless while waiting in line. When Bill playfully pushed a classmate, the teacher reprimanded him and told him to sit down and remain in his seat until she said he could leave.

After a few minutes, she marched the class to the main building for a morning of celebration. When the class returned to the room just before lunch, the teacher found Bill sitting at the table exactly where she told him to stay. Unfortunately, she had forgotten to tell him to return to the line before taking her class to the main building. He had not moved from his seat for more than three hours. She had left Bill behind.

Risky business
(late elementary)

Risk involves uncertainty and the possibility of unpleasant results. Our fear can rise or fall depending on the level of risk. Involve children in a discussion about taking risks using the following exercise.

Take out a pack of poker cards and shuffle them. Choose one card and place it face down on a table. Then say something like: "Let's pretend I will give you the opportunity to go shopping to buy you whatever you want from a toy store, depending on the card I just dealt you. If it is a heart or diamond, you get to go shopping. If it is a spade, nothing happens. If it is a club, you have to give (name *two* favorite playthings) to charity. If you could really make this choice would you take the risk?" Talk briefly about the choice and then turn the card over.

Follow up with something like, "I am using cards here to illustrate risk. What are some real examples of risks that kids your age have faced?" Ask them to comment about the following examples if they cannot think of some on their own:

Being truthful when you might be punished.

Saying "no" when asked by friends to drink alcohol.

Telling some classmates to stop making fun of another kid.

Telling a friend that you feel angry toward him (or her).

Standing up in class to give a speech.

At such a young age, Bill believed the responsible action was to do exactly as the teacher told him, and he had the self-discipline to follow through on this conviction. As he grew older, his sense of fairness and justice would become more sophisticated than simple obedience.

Talk with children about justice

When asked about her earliest memory of being treated unjustly, a friend recalled Christmas morning when she was seven years old. Everyone in her family was sitting around the tree opening up their presents. When it was her turn, she eagerly opened her single gift to find a container of bath powder. Bath powder?

What an unexpected disappointment! Fighting back tears, she sat through the remainder of the celebration holding the powder in her lap while others displayed their treasures with enthusiasm.

After everyone opened the gifts, her father took her to the back room where he presented her with a brand new bicycle. She recalls being excited about getting the bike. But what she most remembers, though, is the surge of sadness and shame she initially felt after opening the "joke" gift in front of the rest of the family.

Her parents were unaware of the strong sense of injustice that their surprise would create. They didn't realize that she would feel slighted in ways that she would not have otherwise been at a younger age. Seven-year-olds are beginning to compare themselves to others and make self-evaluations.

Before the age of five, children reason that what they desire is "right" ("I should get it because I want to have it"). By the age of five, children view fairness as strict *equal* distribution of goods ("Everyone should get the same"). At age six, children may adjust their beliefs of fairness by recognizing that some people deserve more. They consider *merit* in accepting the idea that some should get more because they worked harder or because they did something good. So we can understand why seven-year-olds would feel so awful when they notice a difference in gifts given to siblings. At age eight, children can begin to view justice *benevolently*. They may reason that a disadvantage (e.g., being handicapped or poor) justifies special consideration.[7]

Children integrate these beliefs about fairness into their sense of honor. In a parent workshop on conscience, one mother described recent arguments she and her husband had with their young adult son. He wanted to come home on weekends to help on the farm. His parents wanted him to remain at college to make friends and participate in weekend activities. Despite their encouragement, their son continued to return home to help plant and harvest their crops.

One early morning before they went out to the fields, the parents made their wishes known once again. The son pushed his chair back, slapped the kitchen table, and pointed his finger at this mother. "Mother, I remember the Little Red Hen!" His mother said she almost fell off her chair. In the story of the Little Red Hen, the hen asks a duck, a pig, and a cat who will help her plant wheat. "Not I," they chorus. They do the same when asked who will help her cut the wheat, grind the flour, make the dough, and bake the loaf. However, they all wanted to help eat the bread! The Little Red Hen chastises them for their laziness and greed, and shares the loaf only with her baby chicks.

The young man had the integrity of his beliefs about fairness. Honor made him willing to make the sacrifice necessary to return the love and devotion his parents had shown to him. If someone needed his help, how could he refuse when his parents had freely given so much of themselves to him? The wheel of love had been set in motion.

Use shame and guilt cautiously

In a moment of weakness, children may cheat, tell a lie, or hurt someone. They may also fail to act when they should, for example, not comforting a grieving classmate or not standing with a bullied friend. By the time they are five years old, children have a conscience that can guide their behavior.[8] Their conscience also accuses and judges when they do something wrong or fail to do something right. Shame and guilt are the twin tools conscience uses to signal that there has been a tear in the fabric of honor.

Shame is a self-conscious feeling associated with the loss of honor. Someone whose opinion matters to us feels disappointed after catching us in a wrongdoing. Shame appears at about age three, revealing the first sign of a healthy conscience. For example, a mother tells her three-year-old son not to touch a birthday cake sitting on the kitchen table. When mother leaves the room for a moment, the child climbs up on a chair and pokes the cake with his finger. When he climbs down, though, he tips the cake stand, toppling it to the floor.

He then runs and hides in his room. He knows he has done something wrong. He knows his mother is going to be upset with him. He hides because he feels shame. He can't bear the thought of her unhappiness with his failure to obey. One of my favorite *Family Circus* cartoons by Bill Keane shows three-year-old P. J. hiding in a closet with an open bag of cookies in his lap and crumbs all over his face. His mother has just opened the closet door and is looking sternly at him. His hands cover his eyes. He tells her, "You no see me!"

Three-year-olds have concerns over maintaining good feelings with their parents and show relief when forgiven. For example, if they hit their mothers in a fit of anger, they may seek to be reassured of her continued love afterward. They may spontaneously confess to a wrongdoing to regain their father's good grace. These behaviors show that children are applying standards of justice toward themselves. They know the failure to meet these standards creates separation from the person they disappointed.

Guilt can emerge during the late preschool years and is a more sophisticated emotional reaction to wrongdoing than shame. Guilt is not associated with exposure. With guilt, we stand as our own accuser. Guilt is action-oriented because it pushes us to repair the damage we have done. A six-year-old who carelessly breaks his younger sister's doll may try to repair the damage. He may apologize to her. He may give her one of his own toys as reparation.

In Donald Carrick's book *Harald and the Great Stag* (Clarion Books, 1988), a boy's bragging endangers a magnificent stag. When he discovers that the stag is being hunted relentlessly, he covers himself with the stag's scent and leads the hunters and their snarling dogs away from their intended prey. He puts himself in danger to make up for the wrong he has done.

Both shame and guilt are important for the formation of a healthy conscience and the development of honor. Both can be oppressive if they are too active, causing children to blame themselves unfairly. A preschool child may believe she is the cause of her parents' arguments late at night because she didn't go to bed on time. An older child may think that she caused her father's death because she argued with him on the day he had his heart attack.

Shame and guilt both motivate children to be accountable. Forgiveness with reparation allows them to repair the self-image damaged by the wrongdoing.

Honor bound, the young women of the Danville High School basketball team accepted the consequences of their drinking. Shawn Durrant and Aaron Hall made the heroic choice to intervene in dangerous circumstances to help others. These young people elevated integrity to the higher level of honor. They put their principles into action despite the sacrifices or risks they faced. They would not flee from their post of honor. Helen Keller once said, "Character cannot be developed in ease and quiet. Only through trial and suffering is the soul strengthened."

Children cannot create honor out of vapor. Children cannot buy honor nor can someone give it to them. They must purchase honor and shape the character of their innermost souls by what they *give* in the heat of life, in the trial by fire that each of them must face. Earthly sweat and tears shape their honor from the moment they were born. As the seventh step, honor sets the stage for valor, the most mature form of courage.

Step Eight

From Responsibility to Valor

Keywords:
inspire, reparation, courage, risk
commitment, sacrifices, faith,
failure, suffering, endurance,
helplessness

Emphasis:
Be kind and protect yourself
and others.

Several years ago, a nine-year-old Colorado boy and his mother were driving to school early in the morning on an isolated rural road. A storm crackled around them in the darkness, whipping the car with heavy rain and wind. The car went into a skid, spun, and went off the road. It rolled several times and came to rest upside down in a ditch.

Fortunately, both mother and son were wearing seatbelts. The mother suffered a blow to her head, which temporarily caused her to lose control of her muscles. The boy was unhurt. As water rushed through broken windows in the car, the boy unbuckled himself and fell into the water rising through the interior of the car. He crawled out of the broken window and rushed to the side of the car where his mother was trapped. He reached inside the car and undid her seatbelt. Then he tugged and pulled her through the small gap in the window and dragged her through the water to the embankment and safety.

After his mother recovered the use of her muscles, she talked about her reaction to the accident. She spoke of the frustration of being unable to help herself or give instructions and support to her son. She also spoke of her pride in her son's determination and good sense. With admiration, she recalled what he repeatedly said as he pulled her through the water: "I think I can, I think I can, I THINK I CAN!"

During the boy's preschool years, *The Little Engine That Could* by Watty Piper (Platt and Munk, 1954) was his favorite bedtime story. The Little Engine inspired him with its display of heart. When everyone else had given up, the Little Engine was determined to carry the heavy load of toys and good things to eat over the hill to the children below. The Little Engine acted because no one else could help. The power of that story took root in the young boy's mind long before the accident that morning, and inspired him in the terrifying moments following the crash.

Mighty Heart
Starletter Williams

At daybreak on January 7, 1998, fourteen-year-old Starletter Williams saved a forty-nine-year-old woman from being struck by a train in Gastonia, North Carolina. The sun had not yet risen, and dense fog had obscured her vision. The woman's vehicle became stuck between railroad tracks at a crossing. Starletter, who was in a nearby car with some other high-school students, saw the woman in the stalled car and then noticed a swiftly approaching freight train on the same track. When she realized that the driver might not have seen the oncoming train, Starletter rushed from her car and ran about thirty feet to the driver's side of the stalled vehicle. She yelled at the driver to leave. Because of the urgency, she opened the car door and grabbed the woman by the arm and pulled her out. Starletter and the driver ran from the track and were just a short distance from it when the train struck the vehicle, destroying it.[1]

In this final step, we arrive at the achievement of valor, the greatest triumph on the path to courage. All of the previous seven accomplishments combine to produce this exceptional response to a call for courage.

The Ring of Valor

Valor is a demonstration of power that enables a person to accomplish something exceptional. The word "valor" is derived from the Latin word for being strong and of worth. The nine-year-old who pulled his mother from their car and the *Mighty Hearts* described in this book all displayed valor. Valor elevates the strengths achieved during the previous seven steps. Valor is the combination of power, care, composure, compassion, vigilance, integrity, and honor. Each of these strengths emerges in a sequence of events in response to a crisis—what can be termed a "Ring of Valor." This chapter will illustrate the sequence with four examples of valor:

- a ten-year-old child who responds to a friend who is hurt while on hike in the woods;
- a twelve-year-old who is approached by a sexual predator on the way home from school;
- fourteen-year-old Starletter Williams (see page 187);
- and a fourteen-year-old who comes to terms with a serious injury.

The first four examples involve unexpected emergencies. The last example is a response to a continuous, persistent adversity.

Opportunities for valor are uncommon in normal times. While willpower, compassion, composure,

The Ring of Valor

caring, vigilance, integrity, and honor are everyday strengths, valor is present only as a response to a crisis. The Ring of Valor identifies a potential or ideal sequence of events (not necessarily what typically happens) as valor comes to the forefront. Each of these circumstances reveals how valor develops in a dramatic but subtle evolution.

Opportunity

The forging of the Ring of Valor begins with an opportunity event: a crisis initiates action. Individuals with the capacity for valor don't wake up in the morning and say, "Today, I'm going to be heroic. Today, I will display valor." They face a threat that creates the opportunity. For example:

- Ten-year-old Carlos and his friend Jordan are on a walk in a nearby city park. They are in a fairly isolated and woody area when Jordan stumbles and falls when climbing over a boulder, hitting his head and falling unconscious.

- Twelve-year-old Madison is walking home one evening when a seventeen-year-old stranger approaches and stops her. He compliments her appearance and puts his hand on her shoulder. After making sexually suggestive remarks, he begins to pull her toward his nearby car.

- Starletter Williams is a passenger in a car that approaches a vehicle stalled on a fog-shrouded railroad track as a train approaches.

- Fourteen-year-old Elijah wakes up in a hospital after a car wreck.

Notice

To *notice* means being aware and alert to danger. The primary strength at this point is *vigilance*.

- Carlos sees Jordan lying on the ground and immediately realizes that his friend is hurt.

- Madison senses the danger of the creepy older teen.

- Starletter sees the train and the car at the crossing. She realizes the car is stalled and the passenger is in grave danger.

- Elijah learns that he is paralyzed and unable to walk.

Scan

To *scan* means to increase alertness significantly and focus all senses on gathering information to understand the challenge. Fear enhances alertness. What is going on? What happened to the other person? Who else is present? What risks exist in this circumstance for others and me? The primary strengths at this point are *vigilance, composure,* and *empathy*.

- Carlos looks around to see what caused Jordan's accident. No one appears to have hurt him. He rushes to his friend's side and can see a deep bruise on his head and slight bleeding from a scalp wound.

- Madison can feel the menace implied in the boy's grasp on her shoulder. She is aware of her surroundings. She is in a public place with stores nearby. No adult is nearby to assist her.

- Starletter realizes that the driver of the stalled vehicle may not see the oncoming train because of the fog. The train poses a danger to anyone who might intervene. No one else is taking any action.

- Following a period of anger and grief, Elijah rallies. He and his single-parent mother meet with medical staff to better understand what happened to him, his prognosis, and what he will have to do before leaving the hospital.

Assess

To *assess* means to evaluate the potential costs of involvement and one's ability to respond while managing fear. The person asks, "What are my abilities and how do they relate to this circumstance?" If a child sees a friend crash her bicycle in the street, assessment may reveal the danger of oncoming traffic. If a teenager who cannot swim hears the pleas of a drowning child, assessment should suggest that entering deep water would be futile and dangerous. If she had been trained in water safety and rescue, that choice might be an acceptable option. Courage without assessment is reckless. The primary strengths for assessment are *vigilance* and *composure.*

- Carlos's father has taught him some simple steps for first aid that could help Jordan. Because Carlos does not appear to be in immediate danger, he is free to put what his father taught him into practice.

- Madison realizes that the teen predator is too big to resist and too fast to outrun. A nearby store might provide safety.

- Starletter makes a quick estimate of the time to impact from the train to the stalled car. As the car in which she is riding pulls over, she considers the distance between her and the stalled vehicle. She thinks she can get there in time by foot.

- Elijah meets with his friends and his teachers to shape a plan for keeping up in school.

Decide

After scanning and assessing, the time has arrived to make a decision. *Response flexibility* means having a range of alternative solutions available.[2] As children grow older, they become more capable of thinking of more than one way to solve a problem. This flexibility enables them to fine-tune their responses to overcome obstacles to success. At this point, *integrity* and *honor* are paramount.

- Carlos decides to first check on Jordan's condition, make him as comfortable as possible, then run for help.

- Madison decides to flee to the closest store and makes a mental note of the safest route.

- Starletter decides to warn the stalled motorist.

- Elijah and his mother decide to enter counseling and join a support group. With the help of his grandmother, his mother's friends, and a supportive boss, the mother makes plans for taking off work and providing home care.

No one makes a decision during adversity that is certain. Decisions are inevitably based on fuzzy information. The plan of action can fail. Failure can lead to disaster, but doing nothing also has consequences. Even though failure exposes the error in decision making, individuals can only make a judgment based on the best evidence and alternatives available at the time.

Commit

Commitment is an emotional and spiritual point in the Ring of Valor. Those who respond courageously are motivated to act. They *want* to do the right thing. Although they have made a conscious choice without expectation of external reward, their choice to move from intention to action requires an emotional commitment. They take responsibility instead of finding excuses to justify inaction. They focus all their resources on achieving success. To respond with anything less in the face of danger is to invite disaster. *Willpower, caring,* and *empathy* contribute to this commitment.

- Carlos cares about Jordan and feels alarmed about his welfare. He has to respond.

- Madison respects herself. She feels angry and frightened, but remains focused on protecting herself.

- Starletter feels from within a powerful force to act. She must warn the stranger!

- Elijah wakes up in the middle of the night with a nightmare. He begins to cry. His tears do not originate in self-pity, but in caring and compassion for himself. As his tears subside, he begins to feel hope.

Prepare

Preparation involves shaping one's intention and the gathering of the personal resources necessary to put the plan into action. Preparing might span two heartbeats or take much longer if the danger is persistent. *Willpower* and *honor* are the critical strengths in preparing to act.

- Carlos takes off his backpack and takes a deep breath as he kneels next to Jordan.

- Madison memorizes the predator's face so she will remember him. She tenses, ready to run.

- Starletter takes a deep breath as the car in which she is riding pulls over.

- Elijah knows the road ahead will be difficult. He draws on his mother's and grandmother's resolve and his own spirituality to find the determination to face his ordeal.

Act

Action implements the decision. *Willpower, composure,* and *honor* are the primary strengths that contribute to action.

- Carlos does what his father taught him to do in emergencies. He crouches next to Jordan, careful not to move his head. He peeks inside his mouth to look for gum that could be lodged in his throat. Then he checks to see if Jordan is breathing. He is. Carlos rises and runs as fast as he can to the closest source of adult help.

- Madison turns and dashes inside the nearest store. She tells the storeowner what happened, and he calls the police and her parents. Madison gives them an accurate description of the older teen's appearance.

- Starletter runs to the stalled car and knocks on the window. When the driver fails to respond quickly, she opens the door and pulls her out, moments before the train hits.

- Elijah puts the plan for recuperation into action.

The time from *Notice* to *Act* in the first three emergencies is between ten seconds to one minute. Facing a persistent, long-term danger, Elijah will set his Ring of Valor into motion over many months.

The Ring of Valor does not always stop with a single act. A response may create new circumstances and opportunities that require renewed movement around the seven points of the ring again. For example, speeding cars can appear on a highway after an accident; water may be more frigid and dangerous than a rescuer anticipated. Unseen sources of help may appear. Until the crisis is resolved, the Ring is in constant motion.

Children can be capable of great valor. Consider seven-year-old Erica Pratt, who was kidnapped on July 22, 2002, and locked in an abandoned Philadelphia home. Her abductor called her family and demanded $150,000 for her release. After twenty-four hours of captivity, tied up and alone in a dark basement, Erica chewed through duct tape binding her hands and pulled off the tape covering her eyes. She then kicked open a locked basement door and punched through a window. Neighbors responded to her screams for help.[3] Can you track Erica's movement on the Ring?

Nurturing valor

- **Recognize valor in children**
- **Put misfortune into perspective**
- **Provide support when children suffer**
- **Teach children to use the Ring of Valor**
- **Gently understand and accept children's retreat**
- **Recognize valor in ourselves**

Each of the children mentioned in the previous section had arrived at a point of valor because their life experiences enabled them to respond affirmatively instead of giving up or shrinking from the challenge. Courage and heroism are not spun from the ether or assembled from genetic inheritance. They emerge from a trembling but resolute heart that stands up to fear to do the right thing. The capacity to take this action is made possible by previous relationships that elevated power, love, and hope to a higher level of valor.

Recognize valor in children

I once presented a program titled "Discovering Courage" to a group of about twenty-five Kansas families. The audience consisted of parents, children, and teenagers. As we talked about courage, I emphasized that a person can feel frightened when they do something brave. Facing any fear, no matter how great or small, can be courageous. I also emphasized the importance of staying smart in the face of danger.

I then invited the children to gather with parents to talk about a time when they did something brave. Parents described their own memories of a courageous moment and helped their recall their own courageous experiences. I invited parents to tell the group what their child did and pin a badge on their child's shirt.

I was surprised at the responses from these children and their parents. Every family engaged in a lively but serious conversation. A three-year-old broke away from his family's conversation to share an important experience with me. "I was brave!" he said breathlessly, "I go in the dark!" He was so excited to tell me what happened (to get his teddy bear, I think) that he could barely contain himself.

Cultural heroism
(mid- to late elementary)

The emphasis of this activity is examining heroism historically and cross-culturally. Ask children to choose any nation in the world. Once they make their selection, join with each child to identify and research a hero figure who came from that culture and nation. The hero can be a real historical figure or one based on mythology.

Determine what the person has done to earn the badge of heroism. What was the adversity that provided the opportunity for heroism? What was the great fear the person had to overcome? For example, Martin Luther King, Jr. was determined to oppose racism nonviolently.

He responded to the suffering of African Americans and sought to alleviate the harm racism caused the nation as a whole. He was also aware of the danger he and his family faced because of his activism. How did the person reveal qualities of power, vigilance, caring, composure, compassion, integrity, and honor as part of their heroism? When did they gain these strengths?

Together, choose an event that illustrated heroic valor. Take turns imagining being the person. Trace how heroism unfolds in this situation along the points on the Ring of Valor, as the person

- notices the challenge,
- scans the circumstances,
- assesses the problem and his or her strengths,
- decides on a course of action,
- commits fully to the decision,
- prepares him or herself, and acts.

When the families came back together as a group, parents stood up to announce what their children had done. Although the seriousness of their examples varied significantly, everyone gave each story their attention and respect. A few of the memorable examples were:

- A grade-schooler found and returned money another child had stolen and hidden at school.

- An older grade-schooler defended a younger child from bullies. "If you want to get him, you will have to go through me first," he told them.

- A young teenager reported to the authorities that another student had brought a gun to school.

- Another young teenager had to choose either having risky surgery or accepting a long-term disability. She chose the operation.

The recognition of the children's valor by the group was both serious and celebratory. Moments of recognition like this make strong impressions on people at any age—whether they occur in public or with family around the kitchen table.

Notice that this recognition is an affirmation (see Step Two, "From Community to Caring") of children's behavior, not of their personal worth. Being defined by the label of hero is a heavy burden to carry. Someone praised as a "hero" may feel undeserving of the title, especially if the outcome was tragic. They may believe others expect them to behave courageously *all* the time. So instead of telling a child, "You are my hero," we can say, "You did something heroic, and you made the world a better place for it." By affirming what children *did*, not who they *are*, we recognize the choices they made and help them understand the nature of courage.

Put misfortune into perspective

The way we explain bad events to children has a significant effect on the development of their overall capacity for hope.[4] Since optimism provides the fuel at the core of every courageous act, the way we react to setbacks makes a lasting impression on our children. Optimistic children grow up in families that view misfortune as *temporary*, not permanent. Children may grow up to believe that because adversity is a temporary condition they can influence its outcome. Even children with an incurable condition like cystic fibrosis or diabetes can learn to tell themselves, "I can face this problem. There is something I can do." Even in the most desperate of situations, they feel the pull of action, to do something to influence the outcome.

In addition, optimistic children grow up in families that view misfortune as *specific*, not universal and inevitable. A child sees classmates teasing and humiliating another child. The optimistic child believes the problem resides in the situation, in the specific perpetrators of the humiliation. The teasing may stop by confronting those who do it. They look at the specifics of the situation. Pessimistic children do nothing because they believe nothing they do can stop teasing. They are more apt to believe that if one child or a group does stop, someone else will pick it up. They are more likely to agree with the statement, "Our life is bad" than "We are going through a difficult time now." They are learning helplessness, not hopefulness.

What parents say and do when responding to misfortune will have a significant effect on whether their children grow up with an optimistic or pessimistic view. Parents are aware of their significance as role models. They know their children are watching. Philip Rog (see page 203) certainly provided a model of heroic action as his son joined him in rescuing a woman and five children. Their actions send a clear message to young people: Although an adversity may seem insurmountable, failure is not certain. If they do fail at first, they can keep trying. They have the intelligence to learn from and correct their mistakes. They are not helpless.

Provide support when children suffer

One of the greatest agonies parents experience is to feel helpless when their children suffer. For example, parents may have to overcome their fear and sadness to provide support when:

- their three-year-old has painful chronic ear infections;
- their seven-year-old comes home crying after learning that she was not invited to a birthday party;
- their nine-year-old stumbles and falls during a field-day race at school, and some of his classmates laugh;
- their twelve-year-old is beaten up by a teenager while walking home from school.

Shortly after takeoff on an aircraft, I heard a young child start to cry. She and her father were about six rows in front of me. Her cries became piercing screams. "Make it stop, Daddy, make it STOP!" No matter what her father did, he couldn't make her pain go away. After about twenty minutes of shrieking, the pressure in her sinuses equalized and her pain vanished.

Sometimes we can provide first aid to ease physical pain. In many cases, our first aid takes the form of information and reassuring touch, not bandages or pills. Sometimes we can inform children about the underlying causes of their suffering. We can use simple words to describe, for example, why a child is having pain and how long we think it will last. We can also show empathy. We can say things like:

Mighty Heart
James E. Rog

On August 20, 1995, fifteen-year-old James E. Rog and his father, Philip Rog, saved a woman and five children from a van burning on a highway in Oregon, Illinois. The thirty-eight-year-old woman was one of thirteen people in a van that caught fire in a two-vehicle highway accident. James and his father had been traveling behind the van, and arrived at the scene moments after the accident. They rushed to the van, and James's father broke out a window at the rear of the passenger side and pulled the woman out, despite the spreading flames inside the van.

James and his father then carried her to the side of the highway. They returned to the burning van, and, in repeated entries through broken windows, father and son removed five children from five to eleven years old. Exhausted and burned, they were eventually driven away from the van by intensifying flames engulfing the vehicle. Of those they succeeded in rescuing, the woman was hospitalized one month for treatment of serious injuries and burns, and the children all required hospital treatment for injury. James and his father recovered after treatment at the hospital for first-degree burns to their faces and arms, and other injuries.[5]

- "You have something called 'sinuses' inside your head that hurt when a plane goes up in the air."
- "You feel left out and overlooked by other kids who are important to you."
- "I know you're scared, but you *are* safe. You're safe with me."

Even though such words may not end the suffering, we can hope our child will somehow hear the message. Later on, when the distress has eased, we can discuss the experience to help our child understand what happened.

Explanations are important but insufficient. We have to establish as much physical contact as the child needs during moments of suffering. Hugging, rocking, or simple handholding let children borrow our strength and may be more comforting than our words.

The management of suffering contributes to both empathy and composure and it gives depth to caring as well. Those who experience love during suffering are not likely to stand idly by when someone is in distress. Bert Bochove, growing up in Holland, contracted polio at two years. His family rallied to help him with his illness. Later, he heard his father tell family stories about a grandfather who praised the altruism of others. At eleven years, his father died and Bert became inconsolable. His older brother brought him out of his depression and encouraged him to play soccer and swim despite one lame leg. At thirteen years, Bert jumped into a canal to save a boy who had fallen out of a rowboat. As an adult, he saved the lives of thirty-seven Jews hidden away in his home.[6]

The spirits of human beings are like "fire-origin species" such as the lodgepole pine tree. The cone of this tree falls to the forest floor, where it remains buried in residue. A seal of pitch protects these cones until fire or heat release its seeds. In the aftermath of a fire, in an ancient cycle of forest renewal, new seedlings emerge, and the floor of a fire-charred forest grows green once more.

In the same way, one can only learn fortitude in the fire of misfortune. Instead of hoping that our children never encounter suffering, we might instead show our love by standing by them and supporting them during those moments when they seem unable, as Euripides said, ". . . to bear unflinchingly what heaven sends." As they learn to cope with the suffering that life sometimes imposes, children will gradually mature and develop the ability to support the next generation.

Teach children to use the Ring of Valor

With younger children, our emphasis should be on developing the fundamental strengths that begin with willpower. By third and fourth grades, we can begin teaching our children to consider and apply the sequence in the Ring of Valor. We can use the Ring to discuss how they responded to risky circumstances they have already faced. We could actually show them the circle, insert the key words, and then talk about how our children responded at each point in the sequence.

By the time children start high school, they can apply the *notice-scan-assess-decide-commit-prepare-act* sequence to better manage everyday challenges and emergencies. Another way to teach the Ring is by having our children talk to relatives about their experiences growing up. The points on the Ring could serve as an outline in the interview and an opportunity for follow-up conversation. Our first priority for children at any age should be to emphasize intelligent decision making. We do not want to encourage children to take unnecessary, reckless risks.

Valor interview
(late elementary)

Make a copy the Valor Interview form (see appendix, page 239). Discuss the process and questions with your child and determine whom the child might interview. Give tips for conducting a good interview. Emphasize that some people feel embarrassed about their personal courage and may not want to talk about it. Discuss what "confidential" means and emphasize the importance of keeping the comments private. Consider taping the interview.

Gently understand and accept children's retreat

Throughout this book, I have presented a case for encouraging children to move forward intelligently when feeling afraid. Movement, however, is not always in a straight line. Sometimes the line jags up or down.

Sometimes we have to retreat in small steps in order to advance with greater momentum toward a major leap.

Who among us can be courageous all the time? If our children fail to face fear courageously, they need our support to learn. Instead of showing disappointment or criticism, we can view the situation as an opportunity to gain knowledge and experience. There is a difference between making a bad decision and being a failure. We can correct bad decisions.

Recognize valor in ourselves

Finally, we should recognize our own personal acts of courage and heroism, past and present. During a discussion on courage, a friend shared the following story with me:

My father came home drunk late at night a lot during my childhood and adolescent years. I remember praying that he would not wake me up, would not fight with my mother, would just go to sleep quietly. Rarely did that ever happen. I always knew if it were toward midnight and Dad hadn't come home he was likely to be loud and obnoxious when he did return. By my way of thinking, I was never happy or relieved about his return. I would hear him come in, stumble up the stairs, and start in with my mother in their bedroom next to mine. I was grateful my younger brother's bedroom was further down the hall.

The night in reference was a little more dramatic than usual. After what seemed like hours, although probably less than twenty minutes, the screaming had escalated way beyond my tolerance level. I was tired and needed my rest for school the next day, I was tired of this scenario repeating so often. I was tired of having to get up and calm them down so life could go on. I was tired of pleading for them to stop. What I encountered when I entered their room was an unforgettable sight, my father holding his army pistol to my mother's head and my mother telling him to go ahead and pull the trigger. There was a lifetime of silence.

Then, there was the unexpected reversal. My father then handed the gun to my mother and told her to shoot him if she were that unhappy and miserable. That's when I walked over and took the gun, asked them to please stop, returned to my bedroom and hid the gun in my clothes closet. The night eventually provided quiet, but little rest. The next day after school I loosened the floor boards in the foot of the closet and gave the gun a proper burial. To my knowledge, the gun is still there. We never spoke of this incident—at least to each other. I was fourteen or fifteen years old at the time. I didn't speak about it again until I was thirty-five years old and in therapy.

I think this is more about survival than courage. While both take a certain level of appreciation for life, the former is more basic and probably less noble than the latter.[7]

We often dismiss our heroic acts as inevitable, unthinking, or an act of mere survival. We don't want to call attention to ourselves or appear arrogant. In the example above, a fourteen-year-old girl intervened in the middle of the night to confront a dangerous and chaotic situation involving alcohol and rage with an unpredictable outcome. Images of glory did not pass through her mind; such lofty thoughts never accompany true acts of heroism. Fatigue, fear, and desperation made her get out of bed; but a heart of valor enabled her to save lives.

John Ceriello, a firefighter with Squad 18 in New York City, was outside the North Tower of the World Trade Center when the South Tower fell. In *Faces of Ground Zero*, he says, "After the first tower fell, we kept searching for people. Was I wary of the second one coming down? Yes. But we don't abandon people."[8] John's comment goes to the heart of valor: caring so strong that it overcomes fear. John is not alone in his commitment to care.

Carnegie's view of "heroes of civilization" is also reflected in cultural mythology and folklore. For example, Isaac Luria, the sixteenth century Kabbalist, believed that God created the world by forming vessels to hold the Divine Light.[9] However, as God poured the light into vessels, they shattered, their pieces tumbling down into the world of matter. Thus, our world consists of countless shards of the original vessels that carried sparks of the Divine Light. According to Luria and other Jewish mystics, humanity's great task is to help God by freeing and reuniting the sacred Light, raising the sparks back to Divinity and restoring the pieces of the broken world. In a shattered universe, the human task is repair. Any act that nourishes or joins together the holy sparks of God's original creation is noble.

According to this folklore, this repair is the work of the Lamed Vav ("thirty-six" in Hebrew). The Lamed Vav are thirty-six anonymous, noble people scattered throughout the world whose sole task it is, in every generation and unknown to themselves, to do good for their fellow men.[10] They perform *Tikkun Olam*—the healing of the world through social action, good deeds that heal others and repair the fracture in the world. They do so unnoticed by others because of their humble nature and commonplace vocation. For their sakes, God lets the world continue to exist, despite his general grief over the behavior of humanity as a whole.

Heroism is by far the greatest of all the healing acts. The young people and parents celebrated in *Mighty Hearts* are not remote heroes. Neither are the firefighters, police officers, and others who entered the clouds of dust and fire to do their work. Like the Lamed Vav, they are ordinary human beings with ordinary human hearts—which is to say, hearts capable of great courage, compassion, and fortitude.

Imagine a world in which the Lamed Vav number not thirty-six . . . but thousands. Even millions. The momentum of that much goodwill would surely transform and heal the world, one person—and one community—at a time.

Every act of courage and heroism leaves a trace of itself in the world, an echo that resonates through family histories and world history alike. In the moment of fear, at the point of desperation, when we find ourselves called to act with valor, we discover the legacy of our humanity: We discover that we are not alone. As Sengbe Pieh said in his testimony to the Supreme Court during the Amistad trials, "At this moment, I am calling back to all my ancestors, to the beginning of time. I am asking them to join me, because they are the whole reason I have existed at all."[11]

Bidden or unbidden, written or unwritten, the spirit of courage generated by hundreds of thousands of human hearts over the course of history is with us. That spirit is the source of the might that fills our hearts when we rise to every challenge requiring courage. That is their legacy to us, and it is our gift to our children.

Our task is to fuel the flames of the spirit of courage by adding our sparks to it, and to teach our children to harness that fire to push back darkness and fear. In this way we will light up the world with fresh heroism and hope.

Appendix

Developmental Milestones
in Courage

The Developmental Milestones in Courage are based on reviews of research or the author's observations of preschool children.[1] Use the Milestones as an informal tool to track your child's achievements. Look for evidence of these Milestones in your child's everyday behavior. Since many require conditions that occur infrequently, the failure to observe evidence of achievement *does not* mean a child is incapable of the behavior.

Milestones are learned through everyday life experience. They cannot be accelerated through instruction. Also, not all Milestones are equally important. Each Milestone shows the approximate age at which most children *could* achieve success. Ages for the Milestones are points in time, not periods of time. For example, *3 Years* means "by the child's third birthday." Rates of maturation vary, so the age of achievement is not the same for all children. If you are concerned about your child's development, consult a medical or mental health professional.

The following are Developmental Milestones in Courage from infancy to adolescence.

3 months

Willpower

❑ Lifts head when held at your shoulder.

❑ Lifts head and chest when lying on her stomach.

Caring

❑ Responds to you (and other friendly people) with a true social smile (six weeks).

❑ Responds with sound and movement when you talk to her; has good eye contact with you.

Composure

❑ Recovers from disappointment when you stop playing with him.

❑ Calms down on hearing your soothing voice (three weeks).

Empathy

❑ Imitates your facial expressions of happiness and anger.

❑ Cries in response to another child's crying.

❑ Responds differently to your happy, sad, and angry facial and vocal expressions. She may look away and fuss if you show her a motionless sad face.

6 months

Willpower

❑ Reaches for and grasps objects.

❑ Explores by mouthing and banging objects.

❑ Rolls over.

- ❑ Cries to communicate pain, fear, discomfort, or loneliness.

- ❑ Cries deliberately to let you know he wants something.

- ❑ Shows anger and occasionally resists your restraint.

- ❑ Smiles at herself in the mirror.

- ❑ Shows distress when toy is taken away.

Caring

- ❑ Knows familiar faces.

- ❑ Engages in brief "conversations" with you; her coos and gurgles are often accompanied by hand or finger movements and by a smile or excited facial expression.

- ❑ Expressions of happiness are greater when interacting with you than with someone who is less familiar to him.

- ❑ Shows distinct sadness and distress when put down and left, and then reacts positively when you return.

- ❑ Enjoys your gentle caresses and cuddling.

Vigilance

- ❑ Shows fear (true fear, not startle) of the unexpected or unfamiliar.

Composure

- ❑ First looks sad and then puckers up his lips before starting to cry. Crying is no longer instantaneous and agitated.

- ❑ Shows significant decrease in the amount of time

necessary to recover from distress.

❑ Makes efforts to soothe self when distressed, e.g., sucks thumb or pacifier.

Empathy

❑ Knows by your facial expression when you are angry, surprised, or afraid.

❑ Imitates your gestures, facial expressions, and vocalizations.

❑ Reacts to the strong emotions of others by focusing on himself, e.g., cries or touches self when hearing another baby cry.

9 months

Caring

❑ "Conversations" become more like true dialogue. She seems to be listening to you.

❑ Enjoys playing brief and simple games with you.

Vigilance

❑ Shows fear of falling off high places such as table, chairs, or steps.

❑ Afraid of strangers.

Empathy

❑ Displays joy, sadness, fear, disgust, interest, surprise, anger, and affection in reasonable circumstances.

❑ Mirrors your posed expressions of joy and sadness.

Integrity

❑ Understands "no-no."

1 year

Willpower

❏ Explores by crawling on hands and knees.

❏ Feeds herself finger food like raisins or breadcrumbs.

❏ Puts small blocks in and takes them out of a container.

❏ Walks with one hand held.

❏ Makes sounds or motions to show that he wants you to do something (like raising his arms to be picked up).

❏ Cries when picked up by a stranger who approaches too quickly.

Caring

❏ Waves "hi" or "good-bye" to you.

❏ Smiles at strangers when you are nearby.

❏ Difficult to console when separated from those she loves.

❏ Shows interest in nearby babies.

Vigilance

❏ Moves a blocking object in order to grab a toy.

❏ Appears to be upset when loved ones yell at each other.

Composure

❏ Regulates her own behavior to avoid making you upset (studies your emotional response).

❑ Moderates arousal if another purpose gains priority, e.g., stops crying to grab a toy or take a cookie.

Empathy

❑ Follows a line of sight of your eyes or the direction of your pointed finger to pick out an object of your attention.

❑ Associates a picture of a happy or angry person with the same voice tone.

❑ Observes and imitates others without being coached to do so (with a slight time delay).

❑ Becomes agitated and disturbed when she views others in distress.

Integrity

❑ Plays brief, cooperative "games" with simple rules, e.g., I do one thing, you do another.

1.5 years

Willpower

❑ Walks without help.

❑ Learns what to do with objects by watching what others do.

Caring

❑ Brings toys to show you.

❑ Leaves your side to explore and then establishes contact with you from a distance for reassurance; returns occasionally during play for "emotional refueling."

Vigilance

☐ Recognizes discrepancies in self in a mirror reflection, e.g., touches nose with rouge on it.

☐ Calls attention to things that are broken or flawed, e.g., brings a toy doll with missing eye to parent and points to the flaw.

Composure

☐ Purposefully quiets himself when he is upset. Recovers from anger after a few minutes.

☐ When asked, consciously or deliberately restrains himself for a brief interval (20 seconds) before giving in to an impulse, e.g., opening a brightly wrapped package or snatching a raisin from under a cup.

Empathy

☐ Looks at you when she begins talking with you; tries to understand.

☐ Anticipates your feelings and receives pleasure from her power to influence another's emotions (may seem like teasing). For example, she pulls your hair. You say "no." She says "yes" and smiles. You say "no," and she says "nice!"

☐ Helps someone in distress by patting or stroking, or to a lesser extent hugging and kissing. Does primarily what he would find self-comforting.

Integrity

☐ Enjoys playing longer games with simple rules of give-and-take or hiding-and-finding, e.g., peekaboo.

❑ Makes vocal expressions to express purposes, interests, pleasure, and surprise.

❑ Says or does something to show she knows that some behaviors are unacceptable, e.g., spills drink, vocalizes, looks at mother and points to spill while saying, "Uh-oh." No expression of shame or guilt yet.

Valor

❑ Defends a loved one who is hurt by another, e.g., a seventeen-month-old in a doctor's office sees his brother get a shot and responds by hitting the doctor.

❑ Occasionally makes a sacrifice to alleviate another's distress, e.g., offers teddy bear to crying friend, then gets friend's blanket.

2 years

Willpower

❑ Feeds self with spoon.

❑ Walks up steps with help.

❑ Builds a tower of three to four blocks.

❑ Pulls at you so she can show you something.

❑ Enjoys exploring; gets into things and requires nearly constant supervision.

❑ May get physically aggressive when frustrated; slaps, hits.

❑ Identifies his own photo when asked to find it in a stack of photos.

❑ Refers to self by first name and uses pronouns "I" and "mine."

Caring

- ☐ Seeks out and enjoys simple interactions with other children, e.g., loud chanting or jumping up and falling down together.

- ☐ Brings toys to share play with loved ones (more advanced than just showing).

- ☐ Talks spontaneously about his genuine affection for those he loves.

- ☐ Refers to others by name.

- ☐ Enjoys an audience and applause.

Vigilance

- ☐ Shows caution but not excessive fear toward friendly strangers when you are present; reacts positively to strangers from a safe distance.

- ☐ Makes appeals for sympathy when hurt.

Composure

- ☐ Takes turns in conversations while remaining focused on a specific topic.

- ☐ Engages in a three-way, joint attention episodes involving some give and take among all participants; contributes to the ongoing conversation with her turn at talk (multiple-person conversation).

- ☐ Suppresses negative emotions in various physical ways, e.g., a wrinkled brow, compressed lips, lip biting, based on an understanding of what is and what is not allowed.

- ☐ When left alone for a brief period, complies with a request not to touch an attractive object.

- ☐ Dramatizes distress to get assistance.

Empathy

☐ Understands that wanting something and getting it leads to happiness and that wanting something and not getting it leads to sadness.

☐ Genuinely understands that he and others are independent agents, that both actors in the social exchange are playing separate roles and have separate independent intentions.

Integrity

☐ Plays more elaborate games with simple rules, e.g., run-and-chase or catch-and-throw-back.

☐ Asserts that rules applied to her should also be applied to a brother or sister.

Honor

☐ Resolves peer conflicts by sharing a toy.

☐ Occasionally participates in housekeeping tasks without being told to do so, e.g., boy with toy lawnmower and shovel "helps" his dad.

☐ Stops doing something when asked (responds correctly to your disapproving looks and gestures).

☐ May try to evade or cover up a wrongdoing, e.g., mother finds forbidden cookies hidden in a closet.

☐ Becomes downcast and turns away when you react with strong displeasure or disgust.

☐ Understands that she can hurt others. For example, a child hits her baby brother and says "Poor Thomas." Mother responds, "What happened?" Child says, "I banged him." Mother replies, "Well, you better kiss him better."

❏ May spontaneously tell or show you that he has done something wrong.

2.5 years

Willpower

❏ Occasionally resists authority by asserting his desires, possibly saying "No!"

❏ Talks about what he wants and how he feels ("I want a cookie").

❏ Uses the words "I," "me," and "mine."

Caring

❏ Talks with you about the day's recollections.

Vigilance

❏ Shows a sense of humor; laughs at silly labeling of objects and events (as in calling a nose an "ear").

❏ Seeks an explanation for what is broken or flawed, e.g., may ask, "Who broke it?" or "Who hit him?"

Composure

❏ Adjusts her behavior somewhat when in public.

Empathy

❏ Pretends to be kind to a doll or stuffed animal as if it were human (as in feeding a teddy bear).

❏ Acts upset when seeing someone or something that is hurt.

❏ Offers a spontaneous and familiar kindness to comfort someone who is sad, e.g., shares her blanket.

❑ Uses words to console a brother or sister who is distressed.

Integrity

❑ Recognizes that questions require responses.

❑ Looks to see if you are watching when she does something wrong, i.e., knows she is doing something wrong.

❑ Shows pleasure in "getting it right."

❑ Very possessive, e.g., offers toys to other children, but then wants them back.

Honor

❑ Understands accountability (as indicated by blaming others and denying his culpability). May seem like lying to you.

❑ Makes a sincere apology or offers some other sign of remorse after harming someone.

❑ Makes self-evaluative statements, e.g,, "I a bad bad boy, Mommy."

Valor

❑ Tries to get someone to help a brother or sister in distress.

3 years

Willpower

❑ Places himself in a near-future context; e.g., "I go to Grandma's when Mommy comes to get me."

Caring

❑ Participates in family storytelling about shared experiences.

- [ ] Uses words or gestures to communicate a desire for closeness, e.g., says "hug" or gestures to sit in your lap to allow for hugging.

- [ ] Directs social acts toward two other children at once (aware of audience).

Composure

- [ ] Alternates or exchanges emotional modes of expressiveness as the situation demands, e.g., knows that glaring at a peer is more effective than hitting him or having a temper tantrum which might trigger parental intervention. As a result, temper tantrums decrease by thirty months of age.

- [ ] Purposefully uses an emotional display to elicit adult attention, e.g., after bumping elbow, does not cry until adult enters the room.

- [ ] Recovers from anger or temper tantrum and is cooperative and organized (after five or ten minutes).

- [ ] Hides her emotional state (though not adept at doing so).

Empathy

- [ ] Knows that individual emotional reactions in others will diverge depending on the desires or preferences of the individual.

- [ ] Shows awareness that others' feelings can differ from her own.

- [ ] Engages in pretend play about emotional states, e.g., pretends to be sad or angry.

- [ ] Accurately names emotional expressions of happiness and sadness.

- ❑ Understands that facial expressions reveal emotions ("Katie not happy face, Katie sad").

- ❑ Understands that a person's experiences affect feelings ("You sad Mommy. You hurt finger.").

- ❑ Understands that feelings can elicit reactions from others ("I cry so Gamma picked me up and rocked me").

- ❑ Uses emotion language in reflective discussions especially about the causes and consequences of feeling states ("I miss Mommy. I get sad."); as a means of manipulating the feelings and behaviors of others ("Talk nice Mommy. Don't be so mad."), and in teasing ("I'm going to eat you up and I'll tell Grandpa you died." "You will? And will he be happy or sad?" "Sad.").

- ❑ Speaks with intensity about his emotions ("My kitty gone. I cried.").

- ❑ Verbalizes emotional experiences of feeling good, happy, sad, afraid, angry, loving, mean, and surprised.

- ❑ Talks about causes of events and feelings to draw your attention to a need, to express distress, or to enlist support to achieve a goal, e.g., "Mommy! My doll broke! Make it better."

- ❑ Occasionally poses an emotional expression he does not feel.

Integrity

- ❑ Engages in pretend play where roles are assigned, e.g., plays "house."

- ❑ Takes turns in structured games.

☐ Questions rules or expectations by persistently asking "Why?"

☐ Shows distress when witnessing another's misbehavior.

Honor

☐ Refers to her own feelings, social rules, and material consequences of a sibling's actions when protesting your decisions.

☐ Expresses more pride at success when the task was difficult and shows more shame at failure when the task was easy.

Valor

☐ Adjusts his help to better match the needs of the distressed person, e.g., finds a crying child's mother instead of his own. Has a repertoire of primitive caring responses: hugging, inspecting the hurt, gift giving, protection or defense, concerned questioning, advice, and reassurance.

3.5 years

Caring

☐ Tries to make others laugh and enjoys the response to his humor.

Vigilance

☐ Draws attention to dangerous objects, e.g., broken glass, pins on the floor.

Composure

☐ Inhibits and corrects herself just before she does something wrong, i.e., can stop the impulse to misbehave.

Empathy

☐ Understands that her behavior can hurt other people's feelings.

☐ Talks about past emotions and mental states ("I was sad yesterday").

Integrity

☐ Reenacts themes of wrongdoing in his play, e.g., scolds a doll for being naughty.

Honor

☐ Can be trusted to comply with simple, reasonable requests when unsupervised.

☐ Spontaneously confesses and apologizes to you, without being told to do so.

☐ Seeks reassurance after misbehavior (shows concern about maintaining good feelings with you).

☐ Shows relief when forgiven for a wrongdoing.

4 years

Caring

☐ Tells you about her experiences. Narratives have coherent flow and direction, like a good story.

☐ Knows what he does can trigger a positive or negative response by others.

Vigilance

☐ Displays fear of dark and "monsters."

☐ Appreciates the difference between what is real and what is make-believe.

☐ Labels statements as true or false.

Composure

❑ Separates from you for short periods without crying.

❑ Delays an impulse through selective attention and self-distraction to achieve a more important goal (is more purposeful and can resist longer than at eighteen months).

❑ Adjusts behavior to conform to simple, understandable rules.

❑ Takes turns and shares (most of the time).

Empathy

❑ Judges the causes and consequences of emotions, referring to internal goals ("He wants the toy") and external outcomes ("The toy broke").

❑ Has a systematic set of beliefs about the thoughts, feelings, intentions, motives, knowledge, and capacities of other people, including an awareness of false beliefs.

❑ Accurately uses terms for feeling angry, loving, afraid, mean, and surprised.

❑ Understands that the same situation can give rise to different emotions in different people (weighing multiple sources of information).

Integrity

❑ Understands "good" as opposed to "bad" rules but does not necessarily recognize the underlying justification for rules.

❑ Discriminates between conventions ("Don't talk with your mouth full") and moral rules ("Hitting is mean").

❑ Changes the rules of the game as he goes along.

Honor

❑ Usually is kind, considerate, and not deliberately cruel to pets.

❑ Applies a notion of obligation in relationships, i.e., an obligation to share.

Valor

❑ Helps another child to accomplish something that cannot be achieved alone.

❑ Shares his toys even when parents or other authority figures are not watching.

❑ Responds generously to another in need, e.g., gives a portion of what she has to someone who does not have any.

❑ Includes prosocial themes in play, e.g., sets up a "hospital" in her room and pretends that her dolls are her "patients."

4.5 years

Caring

❑ Cooperates with other children in play and shows flexibility in both leading and following.

❑ Modifies her language when talking with younger children.

Vigilance

❑ Distinguishes between appearance and reality, e.g., knows that a sponge can look like a rock or a stone like an egg, and that clouds are white, regardless of the color of the sunglasses used to see them.

Composure

☐ Cooperates with other children in play (shows flexibility in leading and following) and adjusts to a common effort to achieve a goal.

Honor

☐ Tries to bargain ("I'll give you this toy if you give me that one").

☐ Recognizes that he could have chosen to behave differently (can understand the idea of being held justly accountable).

☐ Expresses a notion of "fairness" when she feels she or others have been wronged.

Valor

☐ Tries to stop others from misbehaving.

5 years

Willpower

☐ Can be bossy at times.

Caring

☐ Talks about what he might do when he grows up.

☐ Forms a close relationship with at least one other child.

☐ Enjoys social play but sometimes needs to get away and be alone.

Vigilance

☐ Knows that emotion shown to others may not be the emotion the person actually felt, i.e., beginning to understand that emotion can be faked.

Composure

☐ Tunes displays of anger appropriately to social situations (not at mercy of impulses).

☐ Adjusts response to accommodate another, e.g., smiles when given a small serving by Grandma instead of whining and complaining.

Empathy

☐ Realizes the same event can produce different feelings in different people; understands that the causes of happy, sad, angry, and fearful feelings can vary depending on who is experiencing the emotion and that causes have uniquely individual effects.

☐ Understands that someone can have a desire even if not acted on.

☐ Interprets emotions in adult stranger's emotions expressed and distinguishes between vocal tones in infant vocalizations.

Integrity

☐ Talks about her personal future; can respond to "What might you like to do when you grow up?"

☐ Speaks up for himself; shows he knows he is a special individual with personal needs; talks about personal preferences.

☐ Evaluates intention to determine the wrongfulness of a behavior.

☐ Teaches household rules to a playmate in his home, e.g., tells a friend, "No running up the steps!"

☐ Invents games with simple rules.

❑ Uses self-indulgent or needs-oriented reasoning in moral decisions—risk justifies inaction ("Don't stop a bully because you might get pushed down").

❑ Justifies helping others by simple reference to the other person's needs ("I gave him crackers because he was hungry"), to pragmatic reasons ("I wiped the table because it was wet"), or to a relationship with the recipient ("I helped him 'cause he's my friend").

Honor

❑ Shows concern or sympathy for others as a group; refers to a group as needy ("Poor people need food").

❑ Uses principles or norms of equity (an equal share) in distributing resources.

❑ Feels guilty about not reciprocating.

❑ Shows relief when given the opportunity to make up for damage she has caused.

❑ Understands and respects rules; often asks permission.

❑ More positive and prosocial when a peer needs help and is alone than when a peer needs help and is in a group.

❑ May engage in purposeful deception, e.g., tells a lie; understands the difference between factually inaccurate statements and outright deception, e.g., points out the importance of intent.

Valor

☐ Acknowledges that another's needs are a reason to be kind.

☐ Identifies external strategies for resolving another's distress, e.g., seek another's help or change the situation to solve the problem. Also identifies psychological strategies, e.g., redirect thoughts, reinterpret the situation, or say things like "He decides to . . ." or "He thinks of. . . . "

☐ Protects younger children.

☐ Understands that personal sacrifice increases the value of kindness.

6–8 years

Caring

☐ Has several best friends at a time (learning how to be a friend).

Vigilance

☐ Bases thinking on reality and accuracy.

☐ Reasons logically.

☐ Fantasizes about rescuing others from danger.

☐ Distinguishes between reality and fantasy—but may be afraid of scary figures.

Composure

☐ Cites rules for regulating emotion in certain situations, e.g., understands to put on a happy face even when Grandma gives her something she dislikes.

❑ Regulates emotion as part of impression management, e.g., tries to stop his whimpering at school because he doesn't want to be ridiculed.

Empathy

❑ Understands that the intensity of an emotion can diminish over time.

❑ Understands that communicating his feelings can make someone feel better ("I know how you feel, Chris. When I started kindergarten I cried the first day too.")

❑ Experiences empathy for others, but still mostly concerned with herself and her needs.

❑ Shows more concern than sadness or fear in response to seeing a film of someone in a difficult circumstance (opposite of young preschool children who react to the fear stimulus rather than to the televised character's dilemma).

❑ Distinguishes between the emotional experience of himself and others, e.g., he feels scared in a situation but can tell his friends are amused by the same occurrence.

❑ Uses words to describe feeling comfortable, excited, upset, glad, unhappy, relaxed, bored, lonely, annoyed, disappointed, shy, pleased, worried, calm, embarrassed, hating, nervous, and cheerful.

❑ Understands that two emotions of the same intensity can be directed at the same target, e.g., that she can feel both sad and angry when someone wrecks her just-completed puzzle.

❑ Attributes his own feelings to another's feelings or situation ("I feel sad because he feels sad")

Integrity

❑ More aware of peers and their opinions.

❑ Seeks parental approval but becoming emotionally steadier and freer from parents.

❑ Uses altruistic principles for moral decisions, e.g., intervenes in a fight to stop someone from getting hurt.

Honor

❑ Experiences guilt over not fulfilling an obligation, e.g., reneging on a promise to call a friend on the phone and later finding out the friend is upset.

❑ Can accept more responsibilities and understands what "a job well done" means.

❑ Better understands how society works in terms of complex relationships, rules, and roles.

❑ Uses correct emotional terms and descriptions of her own and another's pride or shame.

❑ Focuses on the moral consequences of an act, e.g., concludes that a child who appeared happy after hurting someone was worse off than a child who was sorry for the action.

❑ Considers merit in making a fair distribution of goods (6 years).

❑ Apologizes and/or tries to makeup for the damage he has done (6 years).

❑ Uses a benevolent view of justice in deciding to be fair (8 years).

9–11 years

Caring

☐ Feels loyalty toward a group or a club. She may show enjoyment of code language and passwords used by the group.

☐ Identifies with and prefers to be with others of the same gender.

☐ Continues to need the involvement of a caring adult in his life.

☐ Emphasizes similarities between herself and a friend.

Vigilance

☐ Uses good judgment.

Empathy

☐ Understands that the same event causes opposed feelings, e.g., he is happy receiving a birthday gift but disappointed that it's not what he wanted.

☐ Realizes that the feelings of others are influenced by their experiences.

☐ Understands that feelings of opposite intensities can be expressed toward the same target, e.g., she feels both anger and love for her mother.

☐ Provides more effective emotional support to friends.

Integrity

☐ Views right behavior as "obeying" rules set by those in power.

☐ Looks to adults for guidance and approval.

❑ Judges ideas in absolutes: e.g., right or wrong, fabulous or disgusting. Does not tolerate much middle ground.

❑ Refers to personality features to describe someone.

Honor

❑ Questions parental authority.

❑ Feels guilt over inaction that brings about unfortunate consequences.

❑ Empathizes with victims who were previously described in neutral terms or as benevolent, but does not empathize with victims who were previously described as malevolent.

❑ Understands that guilty feelings, much more than feelings of shame, are associated with regret and feels an urge to make reparations.

Valor

❑ Assists in emergencies.

❑ Donates to a needy stranger.

❑ Responsive to younger children's questions and offers assistance, e.g., shows a kindergarten student where the office is.

❑ Anticipates another's needs.

12–14 years

Caring

❑ Looks more to peers than to parents; seeks peer recognition.

Vigilance

❑ Solves problems with more than one variable.

Integrity

☐ Tends to reject ready-made solutions from adults in favor of his own solution.

☐ Works to achieve integrity, a sense of continuity between inner and outer self.

Honor

☐ Experiences guilt over violating a moral rule that has to do with how he treated another—generalizes over situations and draws conclusions about himself.

The Valor Interview Form

Instructions: Choose someone you know and admire. It could be a parent, or grandparent, a neighbor, an older teenager you really like, or even your teacher. Tell the person you are studying how people deal with fear and find courage to do what they believe is right. Ask them if they would give you a few minutes of their time to respond to four questions.

1. When you were my age, can you recall being scared of something? Can you share with me what that was?

2. How did you handle your fear?

3. Can you recall ever seeing someone do something courageous? If so, what happened? Why would you say the act was courageous?

4. Can you recall a moment in your life when you did something courageous? If so, what happened?

Endnotes

Children, Our Heart Work

1. The word "parent" is used here more as a verb that implies what a person does than a noun that refers to a biological relationship. "Parents" include all those who have made a lifetime commitment to provide care and love for a child. A "parent" may include grandparents, stepparents, foster parents, adult brothers and sisters, and other relatives.

2. Kaoru Yamamoto, "Stress: The View from the Inside," In *Children and Stress: Understanding and Helping,* ed. Beverly Stanford and Kaoru Yamamoto (Olney, MD: Association for Childhood Education International, 2001), 19–31.

3. Christine Gorman, "The Science of Anxiety," *Time,* June 10, 2002.

4. U.S. Department of Health and Human Services, *Trends in the Well-Being of America's Children and Youth 1999* (Washington, D.C., 2000).

5. Andrea Cohn and Andrea Canter, "Facts for Schools and Parents," The National Association of School Psychologists at www.naspcenter.org/ factsheets/bullying_fs.html.

6. Brett Brown and Sharon Bzostek, "Violence in the Lives of Children," CrossCurrents Data

Brief (August 2003). See
Childtrendsdatabank.org.

Step One: Willpower

1. Rollo May, *Power and Innocence* (New York: W.
    W. Norton, 1972).

2. Fallon was a recipient of the Carnegie Hero
    Medal.

3. Charles A. Smith, *From Wonder to Wisdom:
    Using Stories To Help Children Grow* (New York:
    New American Library, 1989).

4. Several of the parent activities in this book are
    adapted from Charles A. Smith, *The Peaceful
    Classroom: 162 Easy Activities to Teach
    Preschoolers Compassion and Cooperation* (Mt.
    Rainier, MD: Gryphon House, 1993). Most of
    these activities can be adapted for use in the
    home.

5. "Black Women Grads at the Citadel," National
    Public Radio, May 10, 2002.

6. Nancy Eisenberg, *The Caring Child*
    (Cambridge, MA: Harvard University Press,
    1992), 42.

7. Jacob was a recipient of the Carnegie Hero
    Medal.

8. See "Bullies and Their Victims" in Laura E.
    Berk, *Child Development* (New York: Allyn and
    Bacon, 1997), 589.

Step Two: Caring

1. Nancy Sherman, "Educating the Stoic
    Warrior," in *Bringing in a New Era in Character*

Education, ed. William Damon (Stanford, CA: Hoover Institution Press, 2002), 85–111.

2. Clarissa Pinkola Estés, Women *Who Run with the Wolves* (New York: Ballantine, 1992), 120.

3. Stanley Greenspan, *The Growth of the Mind and the Endangered Origins of Intelligence* (Reading, MA: Perseus, 1997), 50–51; see also Stanley Greenspan, *Building Healthy Minds: The Six Experiences That Create Intelligence and Emotional Growth in Babies and Young Children* (Cambridge, MA: Perseus, 1999).

4. Samuel Oliner and Pearl Oliner, *The Altruistic Personality: Rescuers of Jews in Nazi Europe* (New York: Free Press, 1988), 171–86.

5. David Rosenhan, "The Natural Socialization of Altruistic Autonomy." In *Altruism and Helping Behavior,* ed. Jacqueline Macaulay and Leonard Berkowitz (New York: Academic Press, 1970), 251–68.

6. Keith was a recipient of the Carnegie Hero Medal.

7. Stanley Greenspan and T. Berry Brazelton, *The Irreducible Needs of Children* (New York: Perseus, 2001).

8. Alana was a recipient of the Carnegie Hero Medal.

9. Oliner and Oliner, 249–59.

10. Kathleen Brehony, *Ordinary Grace: An Examination of the Roots of Compassion, Altruism, and Empathy, and the Ordinary*

Individuals Who Help Others in Extraordinary Ways (New York: Riverhead Books, 1999), 41.

11. Eva Fogelman, *Conscience and Courage: Rescuers of Jews During the Holocaust* (New York: Anchor Books, 1994), 262.

12. Mentioned in *The Practice of Kindness* by the Editors of Conari Press (Berkeley, CA: Conari Press, 1996), 24–25.

Step Three: Vigilance

1. "Kansas vs. Sabine Davidson: The Rottweiler Murder Trial," Court TV Online, at www.courttv.com/trials/rottweiler/.

2. Read about the Carnegie Hero Fund Commission at www.carnegiehero.org.

3. Carnegie Hero Fund Commission, Personal Communication, February 29, 2000.

4. Elizabeth Berger, *Raising Children with Character: Parents, Trust, and the Development of Personal Integrity* (Northvale, NJ: Jason Aronson, 1999), 34.

5. Wade was a recipient of the Carnegie Hero Medal.

6. Diane Papilia and Sandy Olds, *Human Development* (New York: McGraw-Hill, 1995), 249–250; Laura Berk, *Child Development* (Boston: Allyn and Bacon, 1997), 388–99.

7. Terreatha was a recipient of the Carnegie Hero Medal.

8. "Life-Saving Oklahoma Third-Grader Makes the Rounds," *The Daily Ardmoreite*, October 15, 1999, at

www.ardmoreite.com/stories/101599/
new_3rdgrader.shtml.

9. American Red Cross, "Everyday Heroes
Archives," at www.redcross.org/
services/hss/newspro/heroarchive.html.

Step Four: Composure

1. Jim Thorton, "The Joy of Fear," *Adventure,*
June/July 2002.

2. Aaron was a recipient of the Carnegie Hero
Medal.

3. Martha Bronson, *Self-Regulation in Early
Childhood: Nature and Nurture* (New York: The
Guilford Press, 2000).

4. Ann Barnet and Richard Barnet, *The Youngest
Minds: Parenting and Genes in the Development
of Intellect and Emotion* (New York: Simon and
Schuster, 1998), 191–220.

5. Mischel's research is summarized in Daniel
Goleman, *Emotional Intelligence* (New York,
Bantam Books, 1997), 80–83.

6. Beth Haslett and Wendy Samter, *Children
Communicating: The First Five Years* (Mahwah,
NJ: Lawrence Erlbaum, 1997), 31.

7. Barnet and Barnet, 193.

8. Bronson, 58–85.

9. Thomas Lewis, Fari Amini, and Richard
Lannon, *A General Theory of Love* (Random
House, 2000), 78–81.

10. Kathleen Brehony, *Ordinary Grace: An
Examination of the Roots of Compassion,*

Altruism, and Empathy, and the Ordinary
Individuals Who Help Others in Extraordinary
Ways (New York: Riverhead Books, 1999), 39.

11. James Garbarino, *Lost Boys: Why Our Sons*
Turn Violent and How We Can Save Them (New
York: Anchor Books, 1999), 219.

12. Stephen LeBerge, "Dreams and the Senoi" at
www.grasshopper.com/dream.htm; Active
Stream, "Senoi Dream Guides" at
www.activestream.com/Dreams/drm3.shtml.

13. Ronald was a recipient of the Carnegie Hero
Medal.

Step Five: Empathy

1. Dennis was a recipient of the Carnegie Hero
Medal.

2. Eva Fogelman, *Conscience and Courage:*
Rescuers of Jews During the Holocaust (New
York: Anchor Books, 1994), 165–69.

3. Fogelman, 267.

4. Samuel Oliner and Pearl Oliner, *The Altruistic*
Personality: Rescuers of Jews in Nazi Europe
(New York: Free Press, 1988), 189.

5. Daniel Stern, *The Interpersonal World of the*
Infant (New York: Basic Books, 1985), 156–61.

6. Ruth Feldman, Charles Greenbaum, and Nurit
Yirmiya, "Mother-Infant Affect Synchrony As
an Antecedent of the Emergence of Self-
Control," *Developmental Psychology* 35 (1999):
223–31.

7. Allan Shore, "Effects of a Secure Attachment Relationship on Right Brain Development, Affect Regulation, and Infant Mental Health," *Infant Mental Health Journal* 22 (2001): 7–66.

8. Oliver was a recipient of the Carnegie Hero Medal.

9. Susanne Denham, *Emotional Development in Young Children* (New York: The Guilford Press, 1998), 77.

10. Denham, 58–59.

11. Doreen Ridgeway, Everett Waters, and Stan Kuczaj, "Acquisition of Emotion-Descriptive Language: Receptive and Productive Vocabulary Norms for Ages 18 Months to 6 Years," *Developmental Psychology* 21 (1985): 901–8.

12. For an excellent summary of research on peers and caring see Nancy Eisenberg, *The Caring Child* (Cambridge, MA: Harvard University Press, 1992), 104–10.

13. Denham, 78.

14. Beth Haslett and Wendy Samter, *Children Communicating: The First Five Years* (Mahwah, NJ: Lawrence Erlbaum, 1997), 37.

15. See the chapter on grief and sadness in Charles A. Smith, *From Wonder to Wisdom: Using Stories To Help Children Grow* (New York: New American Library, 1989), 111–39.

16. Tom Lutz, *Crying: The Natural and Cultural History of Tears* (New York: W.W. Norton, 1999).

17. Ann Barnet and Richard Barnet, *The Youngest Minds: Parenting and Genes in the Development of Intellect and Emotion* (New York: Simon and Schuster, 1998), 165.

18. Carolyn Zann-Waxler, Marian Radke-Yarrow, Elizabeth Wagner, and Michael Chapman, "Development of Concern for Others," *Developmental Psychology* 28 (1992): 126–36.

Step Six: Integrity

1. Eva Fogelman, *Conscience and Courage: Rescuers of Jews During the Holocaust* (New York: Anchor Books, 1994), 161.

2. Fogelman, 259.

3. Associated Press, "Boy Scout Hailed As Hero for Rescuing Burned Neighbor," *The News and Observer* (Raleigh, NC), July 24, 2001.

4. Fogelman, 253–54.

5. Camelio was a recipient of the Carnegie Hero Medal.

6. Larry Nucci, *Education in the Moral Domain* (New York: Cambridge University Press, 2001), 7.

7. Laura Berk, *Child Development* (Boston: Allyn and Bacon, 1989), 482–86.

8. James Wilson, *The Moral Sense* (New York: Free Press, 1993), 141–142, 226–230.

9. Martha Bronson, *Self-Regulation in Early Childhood: Nature and Nurture* (New York: The Guilford Press, 2000), 88.

10. Nucci, 17.

11. Eva Fogelman; Morton Hunt, *The Compassionate Beast* (New York: William Morrow, 1990); Kathleen A. Brehony, *Ordinary Grace: An Examination of the Roots of Compassion, Altruism, and Empathy and the Ordinary Individuals Who Help Others in Extraordinary Ways* (New York: Riverhead Books, 1999).

12. Carolyn Zahn-Waxler, Marian Radke-Yarrow, and Robert King, "Childrearing and Children's Prosocial Initiations Toward Victims of Distress," *Child Development* 50 (1979): 319–30.

13. James Claxton, *Wise Up* (New York: Bloomsbury, 1999), 273.

14. Kristen Renwick Monroe, *The Heart of Altruism: Perceptions of a Common Humanity* (Princeton, NJ: Princeton University Press, 1996), 122.

15. Monroe, 126.

16. Fogelman, 258–59.

17. Samuel Oliner and Pearl Oliner, *The Altruistic Personality: Rescuers of Jews in Nazi Europe* (New York: Free Press, 1988), 178–83.

Step Seven: Honor

1. Rubel Shelley, "A Lesson in Growing Up," *Heartlight Magazine*, February 19, 2002, at www.heartlight.org/articles/200202/ 20020219_growingup.html; Brad Usatch, "Varsity Girls Confront Mistake," *The Caledonian-Record* online edition, January 14,

2002 at www.caledonianrecord.com/
pages/local_news/story/aeeaa3e8d.

2.   Eva Fogelman, *Conscience and Courage:
     Rescuers of Jews During the Holocaust* (New
     York: Anchor Books, 1994), 227.

3.   Shawn was a recipient of the Carnegie Hero
     Medal.

4.   For a free online course on Responsive
     Discipline, visit
     www.ksu.edu/wwparent/courses/.

5.   Myrna Shure, *Raising a Thinking Child* (New
     York: Henry Holt, 1994).

6.   Annell was a recipient of the Carnegie Hero
     Medal.

7.   William Damon, *Social and Personality
     Development* (New York: W.W. Norton, 1983),
     134–37.

8.   Grazyna Kochanska has published numerous
     articles on the early origins of conscience. For
     example, see Grazyna Kochanska, Nazan
     Aksan, and Amy Koenig, "A Longitudinal
     Study of the Roots of Preschooler's
     Conscience: Committed Compliance and
     Emerging Internalization," *Child Development*
     66 (1995): 1752–69.

Step Eight: Valor

1.   Starletter was a recipient of the Carnegie Hero
     Medal.

2.   Daniel Siegel, *The Developing Mind* (New York:
     The Guilford Press, 1999), 140–43.

3. "Girl, 7, Appears Well After Escaping from Kidnappers," Associated Press, July 25, 2002.

4. Martin Seligman, *Learned Optimism* (New York: Alfred A. Knopf, 1991).

5. James and Philip were recipients of the Carnegie Hero Medal.

6. Eva Fogelman, *Conscience and Courage: Rescuers of Jews During the Holocaust* (New York: Anchor Books, 1994), 269.

7. Anonymous, Personal correspondence, August 20, 2003.

8. Joe McNally, *Faces of Ground Zero* (New York: Little, Brown, 2002), 14.

9. Inner Frontier, "Tikkun Olam: Perfecting the World" at www.innerfrontier.org/ Practices/TikkunOlam.htm.

10. Fogelman, 3.

11. For more information on the exceptional heroism of Sengbe Pieh and the Amistad incident, visit the Amistad Research Center at http:// www.tulane.edu/~amistad/

Milestones

1. If you are interested in the original research related to these Milestones, examine the work of Judy Dunn, Nancy Eisenberg, Grazyna Kochanska, and Martin Hoffman.

   For more information about children and courage and for leader guides in using this book with parents and teachers, visit the author's website at www.raisingcourageouskids.com.

Notes

Notes

Notes

Charles A. Smith is a professor and parent educator in the School of Family Studies and Human Services at Kansas State University. He is also an award-winning state extension specialist who has designed a number of parent education programs used by educators throughout the United States. He holds a BS in psychology from the University of Dayton and both an MS and PhD in child development from Purdue University.

Smith has worked extensively with young children, as director of the Child Development Center at Texas Tech University, as a pre-school teacher, and as a play therapist in a children's hospital.

Smith has created board games, television programs, online educational resources, and several websites for parents and parent educators, including The WonderWise Parent (http://www.ksu.edu/wwparent/) and Raising Courageous Kids (www.raisingcourageouskids.com).

Smith has written numerous articles, lectures often, and presents workshops to parents and parent educators. He has been interviewed frequently in the press and for many years produced a weekly public radio commentary. *Raising Courageous Kids* is his sixth book.

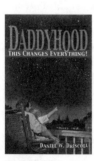